T0323698

Cambridge Elements ☰

Elements in Bioethics and Neuroethics
edited by
Thomasine Kushner
California Pacific Medical Center, San Francisco

PHILOSOPHICAL, MEDICAL, AND LEGAL CONTROVERSIES ABOUT BRAIN DEATH

L. Syd M Johnson
SUNY Upstate Medical University

Shaftesbury Road, Cambridge CB2 8EA, United Kingdom

One Liberty Plaza, 20th Floor, New York, NY 10006, USA

477 Williamstown Road, Port Melbourne, VIC 3207, Australia

314–321, 3rd Floor, Plot 3, Splendor Forum, Jasola District Centre,
New Delhi – 110025, India

103 Penang Road, #05–06/07, Visioncrest Commercial, Singapore 238467

Cambridge University Press is part of Cambridge University Press & Assessment,
a department of the University of Cambridge.

We share the University's mission to contribute to society through the pursuit of
education, learning and research at the highest international levels of excellence.

www.cambridge.org
Information on this title: www.cambridge.org/9781009517218

DOI: 10.1017/9781009323352

First published 2024

A catalogue record for this publication is available from the British Library.

ISBN 978-1-009-51721-8 Hardback
ISBN 978-1-009-32334-5 Paperback
ISSN 2752-3934 (online)
ISSN 2752-3926 (print)

Philosophical, Medical, and Legal Controversies About Brain Death

Elements in Bioethics and Neuroethics

DOI: 10.1017/9781009323352
First published online: February 2024

L. Syd M Johnson
SUNY Upstate Medical University

Author for correspondence: L. Syd M Johnson, johnsols@upstate.edu

Abstract: This Element considers current legal, ethical, metaphysical, and medical controversies concerning brain death. It examines the implicit metaphysical and moral commitments and dualism implied by neurological criteria for death. When these commitments and worldview are not shared by patients and surrogates, they give rise to distrust in healthcare providers and systems, and to injustice, particularly when medicolegal definitions of death are coercively imposed on those who reject them. Ethical obligations to respect persons and patient autonomy, promote patient-centered care, foster and maintain trust, and respond to the demands of justice provide compelling ethical reasons for recognizing reasonable objections. Each section illustrates how seemingly academic debates about brain death have real, on-the-ground implications for patients and their families.

Keywords: brain death, death, law, bioethics, medicine

ISBNs: 9781009517218 (HB), 9781009323345 (PB), 9781009323352 (OC)
ISSNs: 2752-3934 (online), 2752-3926 (print)

Contents

1 Ways to Be Dead

1.1 A Traditional Understanding of Death

For thousands of years, humans have understood the cessation of breathing, the stopping of the heart, and decay and putrefaction to be evident signs of the death of the mortal body. Death may be understood, in some spiritual traditions, as occurring when the soul no longer animates the body or has departed for the afterlife, but the signs of this leave-taking must be found in the remaining body.

Talmudic scholars, for example, "agree that the absence of spontaneous respiration is the only sign needed to ascertain death. A minority would also require cessation of heart action. Thus a patient who has stopped breathing and whose heart is not beating is considered dead by Jewish law."[1]

In some interpretations of the Talmud, the last breath accompanies the departure of the soul. In Tibetan Buddhism, the cessation of breathing precedes actual death – when consciousness leaves the body – by several days. This understanding has long been reflected in the law as well; as noted in *Black's Law Dictionary*, death is "a total stoppage of the circulation of the blood, and a cessation of the animal and vital functions consequent thereon, such as respiration, pulsation, etc."[2] We can think of these traditional ways of understanding and identifying death – or that someone has died – as akin to the medicolegal circulatory–respiratory (sometimes called *cardiopulmonary*, or *somatic*) standard for determining death. The mirror held under the nose has been replaced by the more subtle and accurate doctor's stethoscope checking for sounds of respiration and a beating heart, or the telltale flat line of an electrocardiogram signaling the stilled heart.

There are numerous rich cultural beliefs, traditions, customs, and practices around death, including how death is identified, how the dead and their bodies must be regarded and treated, and how the surviving families and communities must behave and be treated and cared for in the aftermath of a death. Death, like birth, is a momentous occurrence in the existence of individuals, their families, and their communities. Whether viewed as a process (in some Buddhist traditions, for example) or an event, death is understood to be inevitable.[3] While the ordinary, commonplace, traditional understanding of death predates modern science and medicine, and sometimes includes unscientific concepts like the soul, spirit, or afterlife, it is not wrong according to modern science. The body in rigor mortis is without question and scientifically confirmably dead, and so is the decaying body. The body with prolonged cessation of cardiac and respiratory activity is dead. This is almost universally agreed upon across cultures, and across religious and spiritual traditions. Indeed, most deaths continue to be determined by the absence of circulatory–respiratory functions, or the presence of bodily rigor or decay. Humans understand these to be signs of death both in their own kind, and in other species with whom we share our lives, and whose corpses we encounter in the world.

1.2 Inventing Brain Death

Despite this very wide consensus concerning death, and near-universal acceptance across human cultures and traditions of circulatory–respiratory death, there have long been questions, challenges, and controversies concerning death. The ability to maintain life in animal tissues, cells, organs, and even decapitated bodies has been demonstrated since the seventeenth century; resuscitating bodies after minutes-long cessation of breathing and cardiac activity was achieved by Soviet scientists experimenting on dogs in the 1930s.[4] The second century physician Galen experimented with artificial respiration using bellows; the sixteenth century anatomist Vesalius used a tube inserted into the trachea to intermittently ventilate experimental animals, a method that would be successfully revived a century later.[5] The use of open chest cardiac massage, and external chest compressions to restart stopped hearts have a history dating back centuries. Such scientific developments called into question the finality and inevitability of death. By the 1960s, these questions took on renewed urgency. Medical innovations like the intermittent positive pressure ventilator changed medicine, and saved countless lives, by assisting those who cannot breathe on their own. But the ventilator, and another life-saving medical intervention, organ transplantation, created the need to revisit the question of who is dead, and how death is determined.

The problem, put simply, was that with artificial respiration, the beating of the heart and bodily life could be maintained in unconscious patients with severe brain injuries, patients for whom little else could be done. The Ad Hoc Committee of the Harvard Medical School to Examine the Definition of Brain Death, chaired by the venerable doctor Henry K. Beecher, took up that problem, publishing their groundbreaking report, "A Definition of Irreversible Coma" in the *Journal of the American Medical Association* in 1968.[6] Beecher and the committee were animated by two concerns: the waste of medical resources in comatose patients with "*no discernible central nervous system activity*" and no prospect of recovery, and the waste of much-needed, transplantable organs, which could not be recovered from living patients lest surgeons be accused of medical homicide.[7] As Beecher et al. delicately put it, "Obsolete criteria for the definition of death can lead to controversy in obtaining organs for transplantation."[8]

The Harvard Committee described several criteria for "irreversible coma," which they said should be considered death: (1) unreceptivity or unresponsivity (i.e., total unawareness of stimuli); (2) no movements or breathing; (3) no reflexes; and (4) flat electroencephalogram, or "isoelectric EEG," which they described as having "great confirmatory value."[9] The Harvard criteria for determining and declaring death laid the groundwork for subsequent efforts to define whole brain death as the standard for death by neurological criteria (DNC), or brain death. In so doing, the Committee did not address the underlying question of why their diagnostic criteria should replace circulatory–respiratory criteria beyond declaring the equivalence of brain death and traditional circulatory–respiratory death:

> From ancient times down to the recent past it was clear that, when the respiration and heart stopped, the brain would die in a few minutes; so the obvious criterion of no heart beat as synonymous with death was sufficiently accurate. In those times the heart was considered to be the central organ of the body; it is not surprising that its failure marked the onset of death. This is no longer valid when modern resuscitative and supportive measures are used. These improved activities can now restore "life" as judged by the ancient standards of persistent respiration and continuing heart beat. This can be the case even when there is not the remotest possibility of an individual recovering consciousness following massive brain damage.[10]

It is doubtful that a counterintuitive concept like brain death, which requires medical determination, is what was meant by death in "ancient times." While it is true that the brain (along with other organs) ceases to function after prolonged cessation of circulation and respiration, "death is the death of the brain" is not equivalent in meaning to "a patient who has stopped breathing and whose heart is not beating is considered dead,"[11] nor does the fact that something leads to something else mean they are one and the same thing. The Committee's work did not merely provide a new way to identify death as it has always been understood. It reinvented death and defined a new way to be dead with a beating heart and breathing lungs.

The Committee urged recognition that the semblance of life achieved through modern medicine is an illusion – we mistake signs of life for life itself. Yet they arguably make the same mistake – they mistake signs of death for death itself. They also conclude that the permanently nonfunctioning brain is "for all practical purposes dead." That the permanently nonfunctioning brain is "for all practical purposes dead" is an unproven assumption that very much depends on how we define death, of course. So it doesn't follow, necessarily, that when the patient's brain is permanently nonfunctioning the patient is dead. Whether "for all practical purposes dead" counts as really, truly dead remains a contested question. There is no question that a body with a severely damaged brain can continue to live, given medical support, sometimes for years.[12] One question that prompted the reinvention of death was: *Is that the life of a person?*

1.3 Whole Brain Death

A little over a decade after the Harvard Committee's work, the United States' President's Commission for the Study of Ethical Problems in Medicine and Biomedical and Behavioral Research again took up the question of defining death in neurological terms. The Commission's report, *Defining Death*, published in 1981, endeavored to provide a conceptual basis for the determination of DNC and to establish "whether the law ought to recognize new means for establishing that the death of a human being has occurred."[13] Secondly, the Commission sought to establish the "interdependence of respiration, circulation and the brain" in a more detailed way than the Harvard Committee: "Destruction of the brain's respiratory center stops respiration, which in turn deprives the heart of needed oxygen, causing it too to cease functioning. The traditional signs of life – respiration and heartbeat – disappear: the person is dead. The 'vital signs' traditionally used in diagnosing death thus reflect the direct interdependence of respiration, circulation and the brain."[14] The Commission noted that "[e]ven if life continues in individual cells or organs, life of the organism as a whole requires complex integration, and without the latter, a *person* cannot properly be regarded as alive."[15] This would seem to flag their intention to distinguish between the life of a *person* and biological life. They explicitly rejected, however, the possibility of defining the essence of persons and personhood, noting the lack of agreement among philosophers, physicians, and the general public. Finally, the Commission sought to make a case for a uniform law concerning the determination of death to govern all of the United States, which it accomplished in conjunction with the American Bar Association, the American Medical Association, and the Uniform Law Commission, resulting in the Uniform Determination of Death Act of 1980 (UDDA), a model statute that was subsequently adopted into law by the majority of US states. The UDDA provides two standards for determining legal death, the traditional circulatory–respiratory standard, and the neurological standard: "§ 1. [*Determination of Death.*] An individual who has sustained either (1) irreversible cessation of circulatory and respiratory functions, or (2) irreversible cessation of all functions of the entire brain, including the brain stem, is dead. A determination of death must be made in accordance with accepted medical standards."[16]

The UDDA defined the criteria for determining whole brain death. Irreversible cessation requires not just that brain functions have ceased but that they have done so without any possibility of being restored. The statute also requires cessation of all functions of the entire brain, including the brainstem. Thus, brain death can be determined only when the entire brain has irreversibly ceased functioning. Similarly, the UDDA requires irreversible cessation of circulatory and respiratory functions. It should be apparent how the term "irreversible" in that context might run afoul of current medical ethics and laws that permit the withdrawal of life-sustaining treatment, including ventilation that supports breathing, or the withholding of cardiopulmonary resuscitation when it is not desired by the patient. Circulation and respiration are not irreversibly lost when it is possible to restore them – in such circumstances, the term "permanent" is used to define a loss of function that will not spontaneously resume, and for which restorative interventions will not be attempted. Thus, the UDDA is in conflict with clinical practice with respect to circulatory–respiratory death. Clinical practice in neurology has drifted from the letter of the law as well, with the understanding that it is not possible to diagnose the loss of all functions of the entire brain, nor the irreversibility of that loss.

There is no worldwide standard for determining DNC, with substantial differences in protocols and practices (and notably, brain death as a phenomenon can only exist in communities and countries with the sophisticated medical technology to keep comatose individuals with severe brain injuries alive).[17] Of the countries where protocols exist, the majority (87 percent) define death as whole brain death, and the remaining 13 percent define it as brainstem death (see Section 1.4).[18] Moreover, in the United States, there can be considerable variation in practices and protocols for determining DNC, undermining the UDDA's declaration that "determination of death must be made in accordance with accepted medical standards."[19]

The current US clinical guidelines for determining brain death in adults and children are promulgated by the American Academy of Neurology and were updated in 2023. The criteria for neurological death are coma of known etiology (lack of evidence of responsiveness); absence of brainstem reflexes (absence of pupillary, oculo-vestibular, corneal, pharyngeal/gag and tracheal reflexes, and absence of facial muscle movements in response to deep, painful pressure); and apnea (or the loss of the drive to breathe).[20] Taken together, the criteria are summed up as *permanent apneic coma* (which is a seemingly minor but important change in language from *irreversible apneic coma*).[21] The new guidelines recommend ancillary testing – such as cerebral perfusion/intracranial circulation studies – only when the bedside neurological examination cannot be completed for medical reasons, or when there are confounders. Notably, the criteria for determining whole brain death do not evaluate nor require loss of *all* functions of the *entire brain*, nor a flatline electroencephalogram. Some parts of the brain, including the hypothalamus (see Section 2.2) can continue to function under the current guidelines (see Figure 1), hormonal activity regulated by the brain (including that supporting pregnancy and puberty) can continue, and there can continue to be electrical activity detectable with EEG.[22] Thus, current US clinical guidelines depart from the UDDA. An important question is whether the legal definition of death should conform to clinical guidelines that reflect the current state of medical knowledge and ability (which is, at best, a moving target) or whether medical practice ought to conform to a definition endorsed by laws and societies.

1.4 Brainstem Death

Ten countries with protocols that define brain death define it as brainstem death: Canada, Colombia, Cyprus, Greece, India, Malta, Poland, Trinidad and Tobago, United Kingdom, and Uruguay.[23] In the United Kingdom, there is no legal or statutory definition of brain death, but the Code of Practice guidelines of the Academy of Medical Royal Colleges provide criteria for diagnosing death after cardiac arrest and identify the point of death as "the simultaneous and irreversible onset of apnoea and unconsciousness in the absence of circulation."[24] Death can be determined by the absence of pulse or heart sounds for a minimum of five minutes, followed by the absence of pupillary and corneal reflexes and motor response to painful supraorbital pressure. Death is also defined as "the irreversible loss of brain-stem function" as evidenced by "the irreversible loss of the capacity for consciousness, combined with irreversible loss of the capacity to breathe."[25] The Academy explicitly states that "[d]eath entails the irreversible loss of those essential characteristics which are necessary to the existence of a living human person," acknowledging that their definition is compatible with biological life functions continuing while personhood is lost.[26] They also state that "cessation of cardiorespiratory function" results in loss of circulation and irreversible damage to the "vital centres in the brain-stem" and hence diagnosing death from cardiorespiratory arrest entails diagnosing brainstem death.[27]

In practice, the neurological tests and exclusion criteria used in the diagnosis of brainstem death are the same as those used to determine whole brain death: irreversible coma, absence of brainstem reflexes, pupillary and corneal reflexes, cough and gag reflexes, absence of motor responses, and apnea.

What distinguishes the Academy's guidelines is the explicit acknowledgment that they are defining and establishing criteria for diagnosing the death of a *person*, rather than biological death. They are quite definitely redefining death as the death of the person, for which the anatomical proxy is the reticular formation of the brainstem. The Academy goes where the President's Commission feared to tread, and defines the two capacities that are essential and necessary characteristics of a living human *person*, the capacity for consciousness, and the capacity to breathe. It must be said that these are odd criteria for personhood, a *non sequitur* even, because the capacity to breathe is not anyone's idea of an essential characteristic of *persons*. There are lots of people who cannot breathe without assistance and they are uncontroversially both alive and persons.

To its credit, the Academy's definition of death is very clear about what is to be medically diagnosed, and thus avoids the problem faced by the American guidelines of the accepted medical criteria being inconsistent with a statutory definition. The Academy doesn't claim biological equivalence between brainstem death and circulatory–respiratory death, although its criteria for circulatory–respiratory death include neurological criteria. And it is clear about the conception of death as the death of a *person*. Although it is a controversial definition of death, it is a definition that is accepted by many people and clinicians who would apply it to themselves.

The *death of the person* is usually only implicit in the determination and declaration of DNC. The very point of having neurological criteria, or a law defining brain death, or practice guidelines for determining brain death, is that the body remains alive, and thus doesn't satisfy the traditional understanding of death, while something seemingly essential to human existence – the soul, the spirit, the mind, consciousness – has departed or ceased.

1.5 A Single Brain-Based Definition

Recent practice guidelines in Canada promote a single brain-based definition of death, with two methods or criteria for determining death.[28] This is, in a sense, what the Harvard Committee proposed was the status quo when stating that circulatory–respiratory death was always understood to lead to the death of the brain.

> Death is defined as the permanent cessation of brain function (i.e., brain function is lost, will not resume spontaneously, and will not be restored through intervention) and is characterized by the complete absence of any form of consciousness (wakefulness and awareness) and the absence of brainstem reflexes, including the ability to breathe independently. This can

result from cessation of blood circulation to the brain after circulatory arrest and/or from devastating brain injury.[29]

The Canadian guidelines, in essence, define death as *permanent* brainstem death, or the permanent loss of consciousness and brainstem reflexes. What is unique in these guidelines is that they establish the cause as either the loss of whole body blood circulation following a cardiac arrest or a devastating brain injury. The intention is for the brain-based definition of death to apply to "all persons in all circumstances," and not just to those with severe brain injuries.[30] The guidelines also apply to both adult and pediatric patients. But while there is a single *definition* of death, the criteria for determining death vary depending on whether the patient is a "death determination by circulatory criteria" organ donor (referred to as DCC, known elsewhere as Donation after Circulatory Death [DCD] or controlled DCD) or a patient who will be determined dead by neurological criteria (regardless of organ donor status).[31] The criteria for brain death are brainstem criteria: "Death determination by neurologic criteria is primarily a clinical assessment that requires all three of the following: 1) absence of consciousness shown by a lack of wakefulness and awareness in response to stimuli, 2) absence of brainstem function as shown by cranial nerve testing, and 3) absence of the capacity to breathe shown by formal apnea testing."[32]

The Canadian guidelines also explicitly exclude certain categories and types of brain activity that may persist in the unconscious, apneic, brain-dead individual: "Residual brain cell activity that is not associated with the presence of consciousness or brainstem function does not preclude death determination (e.g., posterior pituitary antidiuretic hormone release, temperature control, or cellular-level neuronal activity). Death *cannot* be declared if there is any level of consciousness remaining and/or residual brainstem function regardless of how diminished."[33]

1.6 Higher Brain Death

A definition of brain-based death that has not been explicitly endorsed under law or by major medical organizations is higher brain or neo-cortical death. This is a concept of death "that requires only the higher, or important, brain functions to be present for one to be considered alive."[34] "Higher" might refer to the significance or importance of those brain functions, or it might locate them in the "higher" parts of the brain – the layers of the neocortex – thus excluding, for example, the brainstem, cerebellum, and hypothalamus. Interestingly, the UK Academy picks out consciousness as essential to the life of a person. Consciousness is typically considered one of the "higher" functions (both in terms of importance, and in terms of location in the neocortex) but the neural/ anatomical correlate they identify – the reticular formation – is in the lower brain, the brainstem, so the UK brain death standard doesn't count as a higher brain death standard.

The so-called higher functions that are identified by proponents of higher brain death often include the capacities for personal identity (psychological capacities such as autobiographical memory and continuity of self or a sense of a persisting self) and capacities for experience, social interaction, and rational thought, all of which require consciousness. Indeed, the capacities in play in higher brain death overlap considerably with the capacities frequently noted as conferring personhood or moral status.[35] Importantly, the capacities that are picked out as important can be lost with the loss of consciousness or significant damage to the brain, or they might be absent congenitally, as is supposed of anencephalic and hydranencephalic infants whose brains do not fully develop (although Shewmon has denied that hydranencephalic infants are unconscious or lack social capacities).[36] Philosophers given to fanciful thought experiments would also point out that such capacities would not require bodily continuity of the sort that brain-dead individuals (or hypothetical body-switchers) possess.

Green and Wikler argue that death occurs with the loss of continuous personal identity: "[A] given person ceases to exist with the destruction of whatever processes there are which normally underlie that person's psychological continuity and connectedness. We know these processes are essentially neurological, so that irreversible cessation of upper-brain functioning constitutes the death of that person."[37]

Veatch has denied that death can be defined biologically, and has argued for moral death, in which the loss of personhood is what is morally relevant, and signals the loss of moral standing and appropriately precipitates death-related activities.[38] Veatch and Ross have argued for a definition of death as the loss of an embodied capacity for consciousness, of integration of body and mind, of an entire human being:

> The permanent collapse of the mind's integration with the body is what might reasonably be thought of as death for all moral, social, and public policy purposes.
>
> We opt for the general formulation that a human is dead when there is irreversible loss of embodied capacity for consciousness. This would make those who have lost all functions of the entire brain dead, of course, but it would also include those who lack consciousness – that is, the permanently comatose, the permanently vegetative, and the anencephalic infant – to the extent that these groups can be identified.[39]

There are several difficulties for higher brain views, and for similar views of personhood and moral status that locate those in particular capacities that are instantiated in typically functioning adult humans. One is, quite simply, that not all uncontroversially living humans have those capacities – newborns, for example, lack the capacity for rational thought, as might persons with advanced dementia. Individuals identified as unconscious, in the Unresponsive Wakefulness Syndrome (UWS) (formerly known as the *vegetative state*), lack consciousness and capacities for rational thought, interaction, and experience. But there is long-standing evidence that a significant number of those patients – up to 43 percent – have been misdiagnosed, and are conscious.[40] The misdiagnosis problem in disorders of consciousness is grave and persistent, and although some people do view comatose or UWS patients as "for all practical purposes dead," the spectrum of impairments of consciousness and the significant diagnostic and prognostic uncertainty are serious hurdles that must be overcome by proponents of higher brain death.[41] Bernat, a long-standing defender of whole brain death, cautions that if loss of consciousness is death, then unconscious people who are currently considered to be alive in every society and culture would be regarded as dead. This, he says, "contrives a redefinition of death."[42] The Harvard Committee suggested continuity, if not identity, between disorders of consciousness and death by labelling brain death as "irreversible coma."[43] Johnson suggests that "[o]ne might rightly ask if the only difference between brain death and coma is 'irreversibility,' or the lost potential for recovery," while noting that brain death, because it usually leads to the withdrawal of life-sustaining treatment, is a self-fulfilling prophecy of death – an uncertain diagnosis of death that inevitably leads to death.[44] Self-fulfilling prophecies, it must be noted, are rife in the context of brain injuries, where withdrawal of treatment is a leading cause of death.[45] Also noteworthy is that there are documented cases of misdiagnosis of brain death.[46] Unlike misdiagnosis in disorders of consciousness, it is nearly inevitable that treatment will be withdrawn (or organs procured for transplant) when a patient is determined to be dead by neurological criteria, except in rare cases where the patient's family or surrogates object (see Section 1.7).

Death is consequential. We need to know who is dead. Who is actually dead, and not who is merely as good as dead. We need to know because there are traditions and practices that happen when someone dies, when their status changes from living person to former person. There are legal matters – the reading of the will, the paying of the life insurance, the wrongful death lawsuit, organ donation, and so on – that happen after someone dies. After we *know* they are dead. For much of human history, the key question was whether someone was alive or dead, and not *when* they stopped living. There was little concern

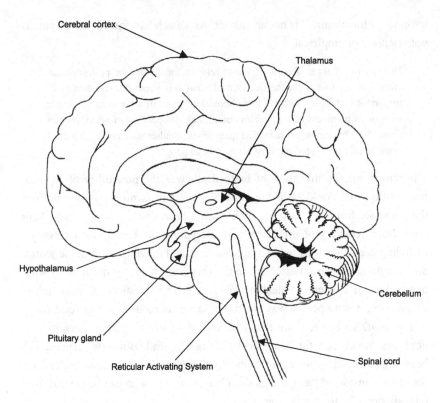

Cerebral cortex

Thalamus

Hypothalamus

Cerebellum

Pituitary gland

Reticular Activating System

Spinal cord

Figure 1 Brain regions and structures relevant to determinations of brain death

with "establishing the exact time of a person's death."[47] Today, the *when* question matters a great deal more, most significantly if the individual is an organ donor, because their death must be established prior to the procurement of their organs. We need to know, then, if an individual with a beating heart and a severely injured brain is alive or dead. Organ donation makes real in a way that is impossible to ignore that the life of the body not only continues in the individual determined to be brain dead but can also continue in an entirely different, separate body. To remain viable and healthy, transplantable organs must be kept alive in a functioning body – their extracorporeal lifespan is limited to hours. The possibility of procuring healthy, living organs for life-saving transplants has long animated bioethical, philosophical, medical, and legal debates concerning brain death, and that debate has since spilled over into concerns about determinations of circulatory–respiratory death as well.[48]

The questions we have been circling around here with the definition or determination of brain death are *What makes human existence valuable?* and *What makes a human being a person?* Those are metaphysical, ethical, social, cultural, and spiritual questions to which "when the entire brain or part of the brain stops functioning" is not an answer. As Veatch has argued, the dispute is not scientific or empirical.

> Holders of all three groups of views rely on theological or philosophical commitments to answer the question of what it is about humans that is so important that its irreversible loss should lead us to treat them as no longer with us as members of the human community. Proponents of all views can share the same empirical data. The question is whether someone with a dead brain should be treated the way we treat dead people.[49]

The reason for the invention of brain death was the possibility of medical intervention that could keep the body alive. There is no separating it from that. And so, from the start, the problem has been that the body can be kept alive when recovery of the brain, and everything the brain makes possible, including consciousness, interaction, thinking, and moving about in the world, are thought no longer possible. From the very beginning, the question of what makes human existence valuable was asked. The question of what makes a human organism a person was asked. Those are not medical or legal questions.

The UDDA does not say that the brain dead are no longer persons – it describes the criteria for being declared legally dead. But those criteria, for being legally dead, or for being medically diagnosed as brain dead, are criteria for being considered "as good as dead" or "someone who can be treated *as if* they are dead," a former person.

The idea that persons (in a metaphysical or moral sense) can die while their physical bodies remain alive is something, clearly, that makes intuitive sense and is acceptable to many people. Many cultural and spiritual traditions contain an implicit or explicit dualism in which body and soul can part ways. The most plausible justification for having a concept of brain death is that devastating brain injuries resulting in the irreversible loss of consciousness result in the death of the *moral person*. But that's not a biological or medical or legal fact – biology, medicine, and the law do not tell us what moral persons are, or when they begin, and when they end.

1.7 Case Study: Jahi McMath

Jahi McMath was 13 years old when, on December 9, 2013, she had pharyngeal surgery for obstructive sleep apnea at Children's Hospital Oakland. Postsurgery, she developed severe and uncontrolled bleeding as a result of which she suffered a cardiac arrest. It took her medical team two hours to resuscitate her, during which time she suffered an hypoxic brain injury. Her brain swelled, a complication of brain injury that often proves fatal. Two days later, a neurological examination and EEG were performed, and Jahi was diagnosed as brain dead. A second confirmatory exam was performed the following day, and Jahi was declared brain dead on December 12. The family was informed that her ventilator would be removed on December 16. Her family objected and retained an attorney, and asked the court to stop the unilateral withdrawal of ventilation, which they characterized as an attempt to kill their child.[50] A court-ordered examination by an independent neurologist, which included a cerebral blood flow study, confirmed brain death. A death certificate was issued, dated December 12, 2013.[51] Jahi was considered legally dead.

Jahi's case generated considerable media, and social media, attention. Bioethicists publicly expounded on the case, declaring the family "delusional," and claiming that Jahi's brain would soon liquefy. Hospital officials publicly referred to Jahi as a "corpse." In a lengthy interview with *The New Yorker*, Jahi's family recounted cruel and disrespectful treatment by doctors at Children's Hospital. In one instance, the hospital's chief medical officer pounded the table with his fist and said, "What don't you understand? She's dead, dead, dead."[52] When Jahi's family requested that the hospital perform a tracheostomy and gastrotomy to surgically implant breathing and feeding tubes that would enable them to transfer Jahi to another facility, the hospital's chief of pediatrics told them: "Children's Hospital Oakland does not believe that performing surgical procedures on the body of a deceased person is an appropriate medical practice."[53] Jahi's uncle took to sleeping by her bedside to ensure that no one would try to pull the plug on his niece. "I just felt her life wasn't worth that much in their eyes. It was like they were trying to shoo us away. They're going to kill my niece."[54]

Jahi's grandmother, a surgical nurse, described a doctor as "all frowned up with his arms crossed. It was like he thought we were dirt."[55] Jahi's mother, Nailah Winkfield, wondered if the fact that the family is Black played a role in both Jahi's death – the family claims that they were ignored when they alerted staff to Jahi's bleeding – and the family's subsequent treatment by the hospital. "No one was listening to us, and I can't prove it, but I really feel in my heart: if Jahi was a little white girl, I feel we would have gotten a little more help and attention."[56]

In an unusual move, Jahi's "corpse" was eventually released to her family, on a ventilator, via the county coroner. Per California law, hospitals are not required to provide care beyond ventilatory support to brain-dead patients, and Jahi's health had deteriorated during the prolonged legal battle. She was spirited away, airlifted to a hospital in New Jersey, where the law on brain death differs significantly from laws elsewhere in the United States. To accommodate religious objections on the part of some Orthodox Jews, New Jersey's law prohibits determination of DNC specifically when there is a religious objection.

Jahi's family had claimed a religious objection to brain death, and stated that so long as Jahi's heart continued to beat, they considered her alive. In New Jersey, Jahi became, as Shewmon and Salamon say, "statutorily resurrected," raised from legal death.[57]

Jahi was eventually stabilized and discharged from the hospital, and spent most of the next four years in her family's home in New Jersey. She and her family were in an unusual legal predicament. Because she had been declared dead in California, they could not return home; in New Jersey, she was legally very much alive, and eligible for medical insurance coverage. She breathed with a ventilator, and received tube feeding. During those four years, she continued to grow, underwent puberty and menses – indicating hypothalamic functioning – and by all accounts was meticulously cared for by her family, and most especially, her devoted mother Nailah Winkfield. In 2018, Jahi developed liver failure and was hospitalized. Her family opted against continuing aggressive treatment, and she died. She has two dates of death, and two death certificates: one in California states that she died December 12, 2013; the other states that she died June 22, 2018, in New Jersey.

Prolonged biological survival following a diagnosis of brain death has been documented numerous times.[58] Where Jahi's story of survival takes an extraordinary turn is in claims by Shewmon, a pediatric neurologist, that, although Jahi was correctly diagnosed in accordance with clinical guidelines and criteria, she later recovered to what was likely a minimally conscious state.[59] That would make her the only known person to recover from irreversible brain death, someone literally, and not merely legally resurrected. That conclusion has interesting implications. Recovery is not possible from an irreversible condition, so by definition, recovery would mean Jahi was not, contrary to appearances, brain dead. Shewmon's evidence for this recovery include his examination of videotaped evidence of Jahi responding to her mother's voice (for example, moving her hands on command), and magnetic resonance imaging (MRI), EEG, and other brain imaging that showed structural preservation of Jahi's brain.[60] Shewmon hypothesizes that Jahi's earlier, repeatedly confirmed diagnoses of brain death were confounded by a phenomenon known as global ischemic penumbra, in which blood flow to the brain is significantly diminished – to a level below detection – but sufficient to support cellular life, and prevent necrosis, in the brain.[61] Global ischemic penumbra is a brain death mimic. Shewmon argues that Jahi likely recovered to a minimally conscious state within a year of her initial brain injury.

One way to interpret Jahi's case is that she was misdiagnosed. Another interpretation is that she was correctly diagnosed in accordance with established and accepted clinical guidelines, but those guidelines do not, and cannot, diagnose the irreversible destruction of the whole brain. The latter interpretation is the more problematic one for brain death proponents, but it fits with the known facts of Jahi's case. It also adds to ethical and epistemic concerns about brain death as a self-fulfilling prophecy – as an uncertain diagnosis of death that inevitably leads to death – for the many patients whose families do not object, or whose objections do not succeed.

A vital lesson from the case of Jahi McMath concerns how we treat patients determined to be brain dead, and their families. Jahi's grandmother wondered: "If the hospital had been more compassionate, would we have fought so much?"[62] But we might also wonder if the hospital would have been more compassionate if Jahi's family had not fought them over her diagnosis and treatment. The latter possibility has important and unsettling ethical implications.

2 Philosophical and Medical Challenges to Brain Death

2.1 Epistemic Challenges

Jahi McMath's extraordinary case – and her possible recovery from death – is illustrative of the epistemic challenges encountered in DNC. By all accounts, Jahi was diagnosed in accordance with clinical guidelines. Current law in the United States requires a diagnosis of irreversible loss of all functions of the entire brain, including the brainstem. While there are cases in which damage to and destruction of the brain is so extensive and severe that it is with near-certainty irreversible, those are not typically the cases where a brain death diagnosis is needed – those patients often do not survive long enough, or in a stable enough condition, for the neurological examination to confirm brain death to be performed. The whole brain death neurological exam takes time and preparation – it requires that the patient be normothermic, so any hypothermic cooling measures used to preserve the brain must be reversed. The effects of central nervous system depressant drugs, including alcohol, and neuromuscular blockers must be allowed to wear off. The patient's systolic blood pressure must be normal, and there must be no endocrine, metabolic, or circulatory abnormalities.[63] The exam will then check for the absence of brainstem reflexes, and apnea, or the absence of a breathing drive. The apnea test requires that the patient be disconnected from the ventilator, allowing their CO_2 to rise, which should trigger a reflexive breathing response. The patient is observed for 8–10 minutes to see if they breathe spontaneously. If "the test is inconclusive but the patient is hemodynamically stable during the procedure, it may be repeated for a longer period of time (10–15 minutes) after the patient is again adequately preoxygenated."[64] The exam for brainstem death as described in the

UK guidelines is the same, although the interval without ventilation for the apnea test is five minutes. As will be discussed in Section 2.2, the apnea test has become a flashpoint of ethical controversy and objections to brain death exams due to the possibility that an extended interval without ventilation and oxygen will induce further brain injury in a patient.

The determination of irreversibility is fundamentally prognostic – it is a determination that recovery is not and will not be possible. Medical prognosis is typically based on diagnosis, and involves an inductive inference – an inference that is ampliative, meaning the conclusion goes beyond the available evidence. Inductive inferences are also, thus, contingent, meaning that while the evidence might be sound and true, the conclusion – the prognostic inference – might still be false.[65] An inductive inference, then, can be probable, but it cannot be certain. Because the consequences of a brain death determination include organ donation or the termination of life sustaining treatment, both of which will result in certain death if the patient is not already dead, it is important to be certain about the diagnosis and the prognosis. Both the brainstem and whole brain death exams use the same evidence to arrive at two similar, but nonidentical conclusions. The brainstem death exam looks specifically for evidence that the parts of the brainstem that control respiration and conscious-ness are irreversibly nonfunctional. It uses indirect evidence – reflexive responses – of the current state of the brainstem to arrive at an inference about its future state. The whole brain death exam uses the same evidence of absent brainstem reflexes, coma, and apnea, and although the conclusion is whole brain death, functioning of some parts of the brain cannot be excluded. In its 1995 practice parameters, the American Academy of Neurology explicitly describes some clinical evidence of brain function, such as the absence of diabetes insipidus (indicating a functioning hypothalamus), as "compatible with the diagnosis of brain death." It is interesting, to say the least, that the same evidence is used to draw two nonidentical, though similar, inferences. Both inferences are inductive, and make a prediction about the future – irreversibility – based on current evidence that is often assessed within days of a brain injury. Jahi McMath was declared dead three days after her hypoxic brain injury, yet some evidence points to the possibility that her brain injury was not irreversible.

Dall Ave and Bernat have argued that in clinical practice, permanence rather than irreversibility is the standard. Here, a short digression is in order, to considerations of the clinical use of the standard of *permanent* loss of circulatory–respiratory function. In the UDDA, legal determination of death also requires *irreversible* cessation of all circulatory and respiratory functions. In the years since the UDDA was initially promulgated, it has been widely recognized that it is both ethically and legally acceptable and a regular occurrence within hospitals to withhold or withdraw attempts to resuscitate patients, especially when the patients themselves have expressed their preference against resuscitation. Determining the irreversibility of cessation of circulatory–respiratory function would seemingly require that attempts at resuscitation be made to determine if heartbeat and breathing cannot be restored. Similarly, technological advances like extracorporeal membrane oxygenation (ECMO) make it possible to artificially restore circulation and oxygenation in some patients, but ECMO is not routinely used (and survival rates for patients who receive it are 30–50 percent for adults).[66] If ECMO and resuscitation are not attempted, can circulatory–respiratory cessation be considered irreversible, or merely permanent?

In recent years, an increasing number of organ donations are by patients who are not determined dead by neurological criteria, but rather DCD (sometimes called donation after circulatory determination of death (DCDD) or controlled donation after circulatory death (cDCD)). In DCD, the patent is ventilator-dependent, and the patient's surrogates have decided to withdraw life-sustaining treatment and donate their organs. The patient's ventilator is withdrawn, and the medical team waits for their heart to stop for a defined time interval without spontaneous return of circulation (or autoresuscitation), after which the patient is determined to be dead by circulatory–respiratory criteria, and their organs are procured. Because warm ischemic time damages organs, there is time pressure to procure them as quickly as possible to ensure transplant success, and "death is determined at the point of permanent cessation and prior to its irreversible cessation."[67] Dall Ave, Sulmasy, and Bernat have argued that "[t]he distinction between permanent and irreversible cessation of circulation is a practical distinction that has no moral significance or implication," and further is "identical to how physicians declare death in non-organ-donation circumstances."[68] This is due to both practical and epistemic constraints: "The practical way physicians determine death is based on the permanent cessation of circulation, while the exact moment when irreversibility has been reached is not provable."[69]

The question that surfaces in DCD – and in brain death – is whether practical epistemic considerations favoring a *permanence* standard should override other reasons, ethical, legal, metaphysical, and social, for maintaining that death must be and can only be *irreversible*. Joffe argues that numerous physiological confounds make it difficult or impossible to determine irreversible brain death, and concludes that "the appropriate criterion for biological death is irreversible loss of circulation": "The epistemic problem: we cannot make the diagnosis of either permanent or irreversible [brain death] because potentially reversible confounders or mimics are almost always present (e.g., central thyroid and/or adrenal deficiency, high cervical cord injury from brain hernia-tion, global ischemic penumbra, and, with primary brainstem injury, total locked-in state)."[70]

As already noted, irreversible loss of circulation may be equally difficult to ascertain without attempting medical interventions, or waiting an extended time to ensure the impossibility of autoresuscitation. Bernat has argued that the standard of permanence is already accepted in clinical practice, and points to the epistemic problems that maintaining a true and rigorous irreversibility standard would create, including, potentially, the necessity of unwanted medical interventions: "Would proving that standard require aggressive medical and surgical treatment in even futile cases before the brain injury could be judged irreversible? Despite the attraction of its categorical ring, irreversible cessation of circulatory or brain function is a subtle and complex phenomenon and proving it is often unachievable or undesirable in contemporary medical practice."[71]

In addition to the epistemic challenges that proving irreversibility impose, the current clinical guidelines for both brainstem and whole brain death neuro-logical exams focus on a limited number of brainstem reflexes, including those that modulate respiration and wakefulness. These are testable reflexes – a careful neurologist can ascertain whether the pupils respond to light, or if there is a gag response, or a grimace following painful stimulation. But those guidelines permit, for example, hormonal regulation modulated by the brain, the absence of diabetes insipidus (in which there is observable production of excessive amounts of pale urine caused by damage to the hypothalamus). There are numerous cases of pregnant women determined to be brain dead who are maintained on life-sustaining support until they can give birth, sug-gesting, minimally, the bodily integration and functioning necessary to maintain healthy pregnancy. Moreover, the brain dead can maintain their body tempera-ture; undergo proportional growth and puberty (as Jahi McMath did), indicating hypothalamic and pituitary function[72]; and occasionally move (the Lazarus Sign, a complex spinal reflex in which the individual's arms rise up and their hands clasp to make "praying hands" is a dramatic example[73]). Ancillary testing, including EEG to detect electrical activity in the brain, or computed tomography (CT) perfusion, or other perfusion studies to determine if there is cerebral bloodflow, are not recommended as part of the standard clinical exam, but are recommended only where the exam cannot be completed (for example, if the patient is too unstable for an apnea test).[74] Ancillary testing is not foolproof, in any case. Cerebral perfusion studies, for example, might rule out blood flow to the brain, which would be a strong indicator of the death or impending death of the brain, but those tests have been known to result in false positives, and Shewmon and Coimbra have hypothesized that global ischemic penumbra is a brain death mimic that results when blood flow too reduced to be detected is present.[75] Satisfying a literal *whole brain* death standard – in which the entire brain has irreversibly ceased functioning – is epistemically challenging, and perhaps impossible to achieve except in the subset of cases in which damage to a brain is so extensive and destabilizing that the patient cannot be kept alive.

One way to meet this challenge is, as in the UK and Canadian guidelines, to redefine brain death as the loss of function in only some areas of the brain, while excluding others. Another would be to redefine it as the permanent loss of function, rather than irreversible loss, to acknowledge the epistemic probability – but not the certainty – of the inference of functional cessation. This would align with clinical and ethical practice, which permit withholding attempts to reverse cardiac arrest and other medical interventions, including surgical brain interventions like decompressive craniectomy. Both solutions must reckon with the ethical implications of what Shewmon has charged is "conceptual gerrymandering in order to maximize the number of [brain death] diagnoses."[76]

2.2 Medical Challenges

As already noted, one response to the epistemic challenge of determining that the whole brain has ceased functioning is to selectively eliminate some parts of the brain – or apparent parts of the brain – as unimportant. One conceptual motivation for doing this is that the role of the brain in the life of an organism is conceived to be that of central integrator, and some functions or parts of the brain are judged peripheral and nonessential to that role. Bernat, Culver, and Gert were early and important proponents of the brain-as-integrator concept as a defense of brain death as biological death, and the death of an organism as a whole:

> The criterion for cessation of functioning of the organism as a whole is permanent loss of functioning of the entire brain. This criterion is perfectly correlated with the permanent cessation of functioning of the organism as a whole because the brain is necessary for the functioning of the organism as a whole. It integrates, generates, interrelates, and controls complex bodily activities. A patient on a ventilator with a totally destroyed brain is merely a group of artificially maintained subsystems since the organism as a whole has ceased to function.[77]

Bernat argues that an extensive set of organismic functions are integrated by and dependent on the brain:

it is primarily the brain that is responsible for the functioning of the organism as a whole: the integration of organ and tissue subsystems by neural and neuroendocrine control of temperature, fluids and electrolytes, nutrition, breathing, circulation, appropriate responses to danger, among others. The cardiac arrest patient with whole brain destruction is simply a preparation of unintegrated individual subsystems, since the organism as a whole has ceased functioning.[78]

No organism can survive the loss of its critical system. With the loss of the critical system, the organism loses its life-characterizing processes, especially its anti-entropic capacity, and entropy (disorder) inevitably increases. The inexorable increase in entropy is conceptually tied to the irreversibility of the process.[79]

Nair-Collins argues that this brain-as-integrator rationale is empirically refutable, and refuted:

Assuming this theory of biological death, the claim that brain-dead patients are dead has been subjected to what some consider a definitive refutation by empirical evidence. Patients who meet the standard diagnostic tests for brain death can engage in a wealth of homeostasis-maintaining and integrative physiological functions, which together manifest a clear anti-entropic capacity of the organism as a whole, and thus biological life; and they can do so for many years. If maintained with common medical treatments such as mechanical ventilation, such patients can engage in gas exchange at the alveoli, cellular respiration, nutrition, wound healing, febrile responses to infection, tachycardic, hypertensive, and endocrine stress responses to incision, and even such dramatic examples as growth and sexual maturation in children and the gestation of healthy fetuses in pregnant women.[80]

Shewmon challenged the conceptual basis of whole brain death by persuasively arguing that "most integrative functions of the brain are actually not somatically integrating, and, conversely, most integrative functions of the body are not brain-mediated," undermining the brain-as-integrator as a justification for whole brain death.[81] Moreover, Shewmon observed a discrepancy between the rationale and the diagnostic criteria for brain death:

Although the standard rationale contends that the conceptually critical feature of [brain death] (what makes it death) is loss of somatic integrative unity, the standard diagnostic criteria do not require absence of a single somatically integrative brain function; instead, they require loss of consciousness, of cranial nerve functions and of spontaneous breathing (in the bellows sense). . . . Conversely, the comparatively few somatically integrative functions mediated by the brain – such as the endocrine functions of the hypothalamic-pituitary axis, the regulation of blood pressure and temperature, etc. – are not even mentioned in any diagnostic criteria, except for the admonitions that hypothermia can confound the clinical diagnosis and must be absent for validity, and that preservation of hypothalamic-pituitary function does not exclude the diagnosis of [brain death].[82]

Against Shewmon's challenge, a second presidential committee, the President's Council on Bioethics, took up the controversy. The Council defined "total brain failure" as the loss of "need driven commerce with the surrounding world". "[A] living organism engages in self-sustaining, need-driven activities critical to and constitutive of its commerce with the surrounding world. These activities are authentic signs of active and ongoing life. When these signs are absent, and these activities have ceased, then a judgment that the organism as a whole has died can be made with confidence."[83]

The Council describes three fundamental capacities of living organisms, which require consciousness and spontaneous breathing:

1. Openness to the world, that is, receptivity to stimuli and signals from the surrounding environment.
2. The ability to act upon the world to obtain selectively what it needs.
3. The basic felt need that drives the organism to act as it must, to obtain what it needs and what its openness reveals to be available.[84]

The Council denies that theirs is a brainstem criterion, but rather a criterion of whole brain, total brain failure that results from the progressive destruction of the brain, for example through edema and herniation, following injury. Nonetheless, the neurological exam focusing on brainstem reflexes is appropriate, the Council argues, for destruction of the brainstem marks the end of the process of brain destruction:

> [A] diagnosis of total brain failure involves a judgment that the brainstem and the structures above it have been destroyed and therefore have lost the capacity to function ever again. In most cases, however, this destruction did not accompany the initial injury to the brain but instead came about through a self-perpetuating cascade of events – events that progressively damaged more and more tissue and finally destroyed the brainstem.
>
> The herniation ... can crush the brainstem, leading to the functional losses that are revealed by the examination for total brain failure. That condition is the end point of a vicious cycle – the point at which the brain, including its lower centers in the brainstem, has been rendered permanently dysfunctional.[85]

The process of edema and herniation that follows a brain injury does indeed frequently precipitate the finding of brain death, even after brain injuries that might otherwise be survivable. The swelling of the brain can also cut off circulation and oxygen to the brain, causing severe anoxic injury. The

Council's description of total brain failure, while it provides a justification for the clinical exam, fails to address the conceptual question of why total brain failure constitutes the death of the organism, in light of Shewmon's critique of the "integration" rationale.

The Council does not rely on the rationale that the brain is the integrator of bodily functions. Rather, it claims that the organism as a whole must be capable of the vital work of self-preservation:

> Determining whether an organism remains a *whole* depends on recognizing the persistence or cessation of the fundamental vital *work* of a living organism— the work of self-preservation, achieved through the organism's need-driven commerce with the surrounding world. When there is good reason to believe that an injury has irreversibly destroyed an organism's ability to perform its fundamental vital work, then the conclusion that the organism as a whole has died is warranted.[86]

The Council addressed Shewmon's criticisms of the organismal integration rationale for brain death, arguing that he missed the point in focusing on, for example, artificially assisted breathing which merely mimics breathing, but lacks "the *drive* exhibited by the whole organism to bring in air, a drive that is fundamental to the constant, vital working of the whole organism."[87] An activity of the organism as a whole, the Council states, must be "driven by *felt need*."[88]

Shewmon countered with a challenge that applies equally to the Council and the UK Academy. If neither the loss of consciousness alone nor the loss of the capacity to breathe alone counts as death (or, in the language of the Council, the loss of the capacity to perform the vital work of the organism as a whole), why do both combined count as death?

> The inner drive to breathe, mediated by the medullary respiratory centers, is of course absent in patients with total brain failure. But it can also be absent in conscious patients with lower brainstem lesions, and during sleep in patients with Ondine's curse (in whom the lack of drive is arguably also "irreversible," insofar as the person will die during sleep, at least without ventilatory assistance). So even the inner drive to breathe is not a *necessary* feature of organismic wholeness. Neither is inner consciousness, as acknowledged repeatedly in the white paper. The council fails to offer any reasoned argument why the combined absence of these two inner drives, neither of which alone suffices as an indicator of organismic death, together should suffice.[89]

The loss of the capacity to breathe, or the loss of consciousness, would together or alone result in death in a situation where no medical intervention was available. There are undoubtedly many such deaths that still occur in the world, but they are not the deaths that are controversial, nor confirmed by a brain death exam. While being able to breathe is certainly necessary for continued life for humans and many other organisms, being necessary does not make it "essential" in the sense that it constitutes the essence, the identity, in whole or in part, of a living organism. (If nothing else, the notion of "essence" in use by the Academy and the Council requires some explication.) There are uncontroversially living persons who are unconscious and unable to breathe independently, such as comatose persons, and persons who are unconscious (like those in the UWS) and able to breathe on their own, and conscious persons who are unable to breathe without assistance, such as those with high cervical spinal cord injuries. What distinguishes unconscious breathers, and conscious persons who breathe with assistance, from the brain dead is that they have lost only one of the two "essential" criteria named by the Council and the UK Academy. If both are essential to being an "organism as a whole" or a person, however, it's unclear why the loss of one essential feature is not sufficient for death. This is not to say that being unconscious, or being unable to breathe, *should* count as death, but rather points to the inconsistency of having essential features that equal death only when combined, but not in isolation. The addition of irreversibility to those losses does not solve the problem (and in any case, is rarely confirmable), but neither does permanence, for some uncontroversially living persons have permanently and irreversibly lost the capacity to breathe without assistance, and some have lost the capacity for consciousness (although confirming that is also difficult, for reasons discussed in Section 1.6). If irreversibly losing one will not suffice to make a living person dead, then irreversibly losing both would not seem to suffice either, unless breathing and consciousness constitute the *entire essence* of a living human, which is implausible.

Criteria for brainstem and whole brain death explicitly exclude certain areas and functions of the brain. The rationale for doing so can be epistemic – it is frequently not possible to confirm the destruction of all parts of the brain. It can also be conceptual: Some brain functions are not viewed as essential to a living organism or a human person in the way that consciousness is. The debate about the pituitary gland and hypothalamus is a case in point. Loss of hypothalamic functioning is easily diagnosed. The destruction of the hypothalamus results in diabetes insipidus, which is clinically observable. Yet, the absence of diabetes insipidus is, according to the American Academy of Neurology, compatible with a brain death diagnosis, the anatomical positioning of the hypothalamus in the center of the brain notwithstanding. A significant number of patients – evidence suggests between 10 percent and 91 percent – diagnosed as brain dead retain hypothalamic and pituitary function, as evidenced by the absence of polyuria and diabetes insipidus.[90]

Two rationales for excluding hypothalamic functioning have been offered. One is that the hypothalamus is not part of the brain, location notwithstanding. Lewis et al., in calling for the UDDA to be revised, note that recent lawsuits have "raised the question of whether the pituitary gland and hypothalamus are part of the 'entire brain'."[91] There is an esoteric debate about whether the hypothalamus is actually part of the brain, based on its blood supply, which is distinct from other parts of the brain. "One explanation for this conserved island of minor brain function is that the pituitary gland and adjacent hypothalamic neuroendocrine inputs often have a parallel and primarily extracranial blood supply which may be spared from the lethal effects of marked intracranial hypertension."[92]

The hypothalamus is generally recognized to be not only part of the brain but one that regulates numerous bodily functions:

> The hypothalamus is one of the oldest and smallest parts of the brain, constituting just 4 gm of the 1400 gm of adult human brain weight. And yet this tiny area contains highly conserved neural circuitry that controls basic life functions: these include energy metabolism, from feeding through digestion, metabolic control, and energy expenditure; fluid and electrolyte balance, from drinking through fluid absorption and excretion; thermoregulation, from choice of environment through heat production and conservation, and fever responses; wake-sleep cycles and emergency responses to stressors in the environment; and reproduction, from reproductive hormone control through mating, pregnancy, birth, and suckling.[93]

The hypothalamus is described by the Institute of Medicine as a "control center," and the part of the brain that "controls a number of drives essential for the functioning of a wide-ranging omnivorous social mammal."[94] It is both located within the brain, and a structure of the brain through which sensory signals are relayed to the cerebral cortex:

> The thalamus consists of two oval masses, each embedded in a cerebral hemisphere, that are joined by a bridge. The masses contain nerve cell bodies that sort information from four of the senses – sight, hearing, taste, and touch – and relay it to the cerebral cortex. (Only the sense of smell sends signals directly to the cortex, bypassing the thalamus.) Sensations of pain, temperature, and pressure are also relayed through the thalamus, as are the nerve impulses from the cerebral hemispheres that initiate voluntary movement.[95]

Nair-Collins and Miller argue that the hypothalamus and pituitary gland are undoubtedly part of the brain, as evidenced by their developmental origins:

> It is an indisputable scientific fact that the hypothalamus is part of the brain and that one of its vital functions is to regulate plasma osmolality. Similarly, the posterior pituitary, or neurohypophysis, is a part of the brain. It arises embryologically from the floor of the developing ventricular system and is

anatomically composed of the axons of magnocellular neurons whose cell bodies lie in hypothalamic nuclei.[96]

The other justification for excluding the hypothalamus is that, while it is part of the brain, its function is not important, its many vital functions notwithstanding. If we accept that the rationale for accepting brain death is that it is the loss of the brain as "central integrator" of the organism, and that the whole brain-dead organism is thus disintegrated, then excluding the hypothalamus, which serves to control and modulate so many important bodily functions (including temperature regulation, autonomic nervous system responses and hormonal responses, and sleep), is even more perplexing. Shewmon has argued that "[t]o exclude hypothalamic function as irrelevant to the distinction between organismal life and death is ad hoc and simply conceptual gerrymandering."[97]

The position of the American Academy of Neurology's Ethics, Law & Humanities Committee is that "this isolated preserved hypothalamic neurosecretory function is inconsequential and remains fully consistent with brain death by fulfilling the AAN test battery."[98] Bernat affirms that this position "reflects a consensus within the neurology professional community."[99]

Bernat suggests that a slight conceptual shift, from "whole brain death" to "brain-as-a-whole death," could accommodate the exclusion of brain regions and functions that are unimportant, per neurological consensus:

> While the brain-as-a-whole criterion remains in an early stage of refinement, it probably entails cessation of all major brain functions required by the whole-brain criterion, particularly those of the brainstem, but not of relatively minor functions such as hypothalamic neurosecretion and, perhaps, random, disorganized EEG activity. ... An additional benefit of the whole-brain criterion modification approach is that it better aligns the criterion of death with how many neurologists personally conceptualize brain death – as requiring the cessation of most but not all brain functions.[100]

What is certain in the hypothalamus debate is that if the hypothalamus is part of the brain (as has long been scientifically held), and a whole brain death criterion requires cessation of *all* functions of the *entire* brain, then many patients – the majority perhaps – currently determined to be brain dead with a functioning hypothalamus are not, in fact, dead. This would have clear and serious practical, ethical, and legal implications, including that these patients are not legally dead when their organs are removed.

One further medical challenge to the determination of brain death that is practical rather than conceptual is the apnea test. As described in Section 2.1, the apnea test requires that a ventilator-dependent patient be removed from the ventilator for several minutes to determine if they can breathe spontaneously. Under ordinary circumstances, removing ventilatory support from a patient who needs it to breathe will result in their death, either by cardiac arrest or by causing an anoxic brain injury. If a patient is determined to be brain dead, withdrawal of ventilatory support will eventually occur (in those jurisdictions where brain death is recognized as legal death, and which permit withdrawal of ventilation). There is debate within medicine about the safety of the apnea test, in particular for patients who are not brain dead.

Patient surrogates who object to the diagnostic procedures used to determine brain death frequently object to the apnea test in particular – motivated by the risks, or by the potential to forestall the determination of brain death – which has led to legal challenges and bioethical debate about whether consent is required for the brain death exam.

Typically, when diagnostic procedures involve medical risks to a patient, those risks can be justified because the diagnosis will benefit the patient, and because the patient consents to the risks. In emergency situations in which a patient is unable to consent to treatment or diagnosis, presumed consent is both legally and ethically permissible, on the assumption that most people want medical treatment in emergencies. For hospitalized patients, general consent typically covers routine procedures such as checking vital signs and blood draws, but patients retain the legal and moral right to refuse these and any other tests, procedures, and treatments. Procedural risks should, of course, always be minimized to avoid causing unnecessary harm to patients. The apnea test, as part of the brain death examination, never directly and therapeutically benefits a patient, and is not performed in emergencies (as discussed in Section 2.1, the examination requires extensive preparation, and is never done on the fly). Cessation of treatment follows a positive diagnosis of brain death. When the patient's surrogates see withdrawal of treatment as a harm, "the argument in favor of a benefit fails."[101] As Berkowitz and Garrett note: "Because physicians have no duty to treat a patient after declaration of death, physiologic support, including mechanical ventilation, is discontinued without family consent immediately after death declaration or after a brief period of reasonable accommodation."[102]

Numerous studies have identified adverse events during the apnea test, including hypotension, hypoxemia, acidosis, hypercapnia, increased intracranial pressure, pulmonary hypotension, cardiac arrhythmia, cardiac arrest, and pneumothorax.[103]

Truog and Tasker describe the gravest medical risk of the apnea test – that it might actually cause brain death:

In addition to the risk of complications that may result in immediate harm to the patient, the apnea test may confer a more insidious risk, that is, the risk associated with an acute rise in partial pressure of carbon dioxide and consequent cardiovascular changes, which may result in a further rise in intracranial pressure. . . . Such elevation is an important marker of secondary brain injury in patients who have suffered neurologic insults. More importantly for this discussion, however, is the fact that changes in cerebral hemodynamics and hydrodynamics may not result in an immediately recognized complication, but may cause secondary injury such that patients who do not meet the criteria for brain death on initial testing might subsequently be made brain dead as a result of the testing.[104]

Joffe et al. argue against the apnea test, noting numerous confounders, including some not routinely excluded before the test is performed, such as high cervical spinal cord injury and endocrine dysfunction.[105] They also raise the possibility that the apnea test will induce further brain injury, adding a second way – aside from the withdrawal of life-sustaining treatment – that the diagnosis of brain death might result in a self-fulfilling prophecy:

[I]t is logical to assert that an apnea test is potentially very dangerous to a recently injured brain that has high intracranial pressure. Indeed, it is reasonable to suggest that the apnea test itself can result in failing the apnea test, creating a self-fulfilling prophecy. During the apnea test, the rising partial pressure of arterial carbon dioxide causes an acute rise in intracranial pressure in any remaining perfused brain, and this in turn will worsen brain ischemia and complete any evolving herniation, reducing the function of any affected brain.[106]

Lewis and Greer argue that the risk exists, but imply that it is not meaningful because the patient already has a catastrophic brain injury:

Although there is a theoretical risk that a rise in $PaCO_2$ could be harmful, this risk is not clinically meaningful because of the extent of injury present prior to the apnea test. By definition, a patient being evaluated for brain death has suffered a neurologic catastrophe with no hope for recovery. To perform an apnea test otherwise would most certainly be unethical.[107]

Truog and Tasker, and Joffe et al., charge that the apnea test for brain death can be self-fulfilling. Lewis and Greer appear to counter that by arguing that it is merely self-confirming – that it's a test only performed on likely brain-dead patients. It is certainly true that brain death examinations are not performed routinely on *every* patient with a brain injury, but are only done to confirm a strong suspicion that the patient meets criteria for neurological death. Nonetheless, if mere suspicion were sufficient, there would be no need for the neurological examination at all. The concern is that apnea test presents the risk of serious harm – including life-threatening harm – to a patient who already has a severe brain injury. That the patient is already in a life-threatening condition is not a sufficient justification for imposing further nontherapeutic, life-threatening harms that do not benefit the patient.

A critical bioethical question concerning the apnea test, which has spilled over into legal actions, is whether the consent of a patient's surrogate is needed to perform the brain death examination, and, in particular, the apnea test, or ancillary tests. Pope has catalogued legal cases concerning this question, and the lack of legal consensus in diverging legal decisions.[108] Since the widely publicized legal case involving Jahi McMath, the number of legal challenges to determinations of brain death has increased in the United States and elsewhere, and numerous challenges have focused on refusal of consent for apnea testing.

> [S]ome families have focused their legal challenges based on their "pre-brain-death" rights when they still have them, by seeking court injunctions to prevent clinicians from performing the apnea test on their critically ill family members. This legal tactic can, if successful, logistically halt the [determination of death by neurological criteria] and achieve the family's goal of keeping their loved one on life support because brain death cannot be diagnosed without the apnea test. The ultimate result in such cases is that the patient will be kept in the intensive care unit (ICU) until death is declared on the basis of cardiopulmonary criteria.[109]

At present, it is not routine to seek consent for the brain death examination, including the apnea test, in the United States, and indeed, brain death exams and subsequent withdrawal of medical treatment are an area where unilateral decisions by medical staff frequently prevail, both in the United States and in the United Kingdom. Truog et al. argue that the circumstances of the brain death exam require consent:

> Patients provide a general consent to treatment at the time of admission, and this covers all tests and procedures where we can reasonably assume that the patient would regard the benefits of the procedure as sufficient to outweigh any risks or harms. But whenever we cannot safely assume that the patient would want the procedure, we have an ethical and legal obligation to seek the informed consent of the patient or surrogate. Since apnea testing offers no therapeutic benefit to the patient, and may in fact involve potentially life-threatening risks and harms, consent for the procedure would seem to be essential.[110]

Berkowitz and Garrett agree, and further note that it is unlikely that performing an apnea test without consent would pass legal muster:

Ultimately, apnea testing not only fails to benefit a patient in any healing sense, but it risks actual harm, including potentially worsening brain injury or even rendering a patient brain-dead who had not been so prior to the test. The gravity of these risks alone makes the ethical and legal case for consent compelling. ... Simply put, whatever interest the state may have in expediting the diagnosis of death, presumably to facilitate organ donation and reallocate scarce resources, would not constitute a "compelling interest" sufficient to override the objections of a patient's surrogate.[111]

The practice of not seeking or obtaining consent for the brain death examination sows distrust among patients and families, particularly within historically and currently marginalized and exploited communities whose members have well-founded reasons to distrust medical providers:

Obtaining informed consent is an ethical imperative in medicine. It is a cornerstone of creating and maintaining trust in medical treatment and providers. Asking for consent, either from patients or their surrogates, respects persons and their autonomy, and importantly, shows respect in a way that can help foster the development of trust. ... There should be no exception to the rule that consent is required, when a surrogate is available, for apnea testing to confirm DNC.[112]

Lewis and Greer argue against requiring consent on consequentialist grounds, noting the totality of the implications of the brain death exam:

Respect for autonomy must be balanced with beneficence (the need to provide a greater amount of clinical good vs harm) and the consequences of testing for the patient, the family, other patients, and staff members.

A determination of death should not represent a choice. A person is either alive or dead, and delay of this determination affects the patient, the family, society, and hospital personnel. It is necessary to know whether a patient is alive or dead in order to triage allocation of resources including physician time and energy, medications, medical equipment, and ICU beds. In addition, there are nonmedical consequences to the determination of death such as the initiation of mourning, criminal prosecution, inheritance, taxation, and preparation of the cadaver for burial. Furthermore, ongoing treatment after death, outside of the setting of organ donation, can be seen as a violation of a patient's dignity and bodily integrity.[113]

In the United Kingdom, the case of Archie Battersbee, a 12-year-old boy who accidentally strangled himself while apparently doing an online challenge, was the subject of a months-long legal battle between his family and the Royal London Hospital. His family initially asked a court to block the brainstem death exam.[114] Their request was denied, and the judge ruled that the examination would be in the child's best interests.[115] The boy was eventually determined to be brain dead, and his family's numerous legal challenges to stop the withdrawal of life-sustaining treatment were denied. In the United States, several legal challenges to brain death examinations have resulted in a mixed legal landscape, where consent is required in some states, but not in others. In response to the case of Aden Hailu (see Section 2.4), the state of Nevada changed its death statute so that consent for the brain death exam is not required.

The apnea test raises specific ethical concerns as a consequence of the risks of the exam. Those include concerns focused on consent and patient/surrogate autonomy, and rights to refuse unwanted, nontherapeutic medical interventions. While some view the examination to confirm a diagnosis of death as one for which consent is not required, others argue that the apnea test presents risks above and beyond those of the brain death exam generally.[116] And, as Shewmon notes, "it is doubtful that any proxy, after being truly informed about the procedure, would ever consent to it."[117] That, of course, is not a reason not to seek consent for a medical procedure – to proceed without consent simply because consent would not be given would be objectionably paternalistic.

2.3 Ethical Challenges

Beyond the potential risks of the apnea test and the brain death examination generally, there are other ethical challenges to brain death. Brain death is rare, and accounts for only about 1–2 percent of hospital deaths in the United States, and 2–3 percent in the European Union.[118] Despite its rarity, the number and frequency of objections and legal challenges to declarations of brain death are increasing, as has attention to these challenges. These ethical and legal challenges are motivated by the medicolegal implications of brain death, which are particularly onerous:

> It is not surprising that death by neurologic criteria is contested when it is viewed as a way of determining what is only implicit in the law – the transformation of a person with rights, a subject of justice, into a nonperson who no longer has rights. It is not surprising that it engenders distrust because the law, and other human institutions, have historically and frequently been morally wrong in their recognition of who is and is not a person with rights.[119]

The UK Academy explicitly states that brainstem criteria pick out the death of the *person*, a position that was tacitly endorsed by the 1981 President's Commission, the President's Council on Bioethics, and the Harvard Committee. Defining the death of personhood is the motive for brain death criteria, and also defines the problems brain death criteria purport to solve:

> The *death of the person* is implicit in the determination and declaration of death by neurologic criteria. Death by neurologic criteria was meant to solve the problems created when a patient could be kept alive despite the fact that

recovery of the injured brain and its associated functions (including consciousness, interaction, thought, movement about the world) were no longer thought to be possible. That this is viewed as a problem implies an ideological commitment, a value judgment about what makes human existence valuable and what makes a human being a person.[120]

As discussed in Section 1, traditional understandings of death frequently have spiritual and cultural underpinnings. While death is a universal part of human existence, brain death is not universally accepted or endorsed among human individuals or communities, and numerous religious sects and traditions, including Orthodox Judaism, Buddhism, some Muslim sects, and some Indigenous spiritual traditions, among others, reject brain death as death. Moreover, brain death is deeply counterintuitive: The brain-dead individual's body remains warm to the touch, moves spontaneously, and retains many biological functions, including heartbeat and circulation, digestion and excretion, homeostasis, pregnancy, growth and maturation, and hormonal and immunological functions.

Furthermore, definitions of death that are socially, culturally, spiritually, and personally unacceptable impose a particular unendorsed worldview on patients and their families, and transform a living person into a former person. That these determinations of death are also accompanied by requests for organ donations, or in some cases, by the procurement of organs even when the family objects to organ donation (see Section 3.5) creates the impression that the patient is no longer viewed as a person who matters in their own right, as someone with inherent value. The shift in language from "life-support" to "organ support" that follows from a determination of brain death has this effect, and is a stark example of how determinations of brain death precipitate the suspension of patient-centered care, even when family members still view their loved one as a person and a patient:

> It shifts the locus of ethical concern from the individual patient – now a former person/patient – to the needs of others, such as potential organ recipients who might benefit from the act of "organ support." . . . It instrumentalizes patients in a way that would be frankly objectionable if they were considered persons. It is not surprising, then, that surrogates and families might object to the instrumentalization, dehumanization, and downgrading of their loved ones into a collection of organs when their values and beliefs are inconsistent with viewing persons as reducible to brains-that-support-consciousness.[121]

2.4 Case Study: Aden Hailu

Aden Hailu was a 20-year-old college student in April 2015, when she went to Saint Mary's Regional Medical Center in Nevada with stomach pain. During exploratory abdominal surgery, doctors removed her appendix. But something went wrong, and Hailu never woke up. For nine months, her father, Fanuel Gebreyes, fought in the courts to force doctors to treat his daughter. She was declared brain dead two months after her surgery. Independent doctors who examined Hailu did not agree that she was brain dead.[122]

Nevada, like most US states, adopted the UDDA into law decades ago. The UDDA states that "[a] determination of death must be made in accordance with accepted medical standards."[123] Saint Mary's claimed that it followed the guidelines of the American Academy of Neurology in determining that Hailu was dead. In November 2015, six months after she was declared dead, Nevada's Supreme Court ruled unanimously that the hospital had not declared death in accordance with Nevada's legal statute NRS 451.007 that requires irreversible cessation of all functions of the entire brain:

> Here, we are asked to decide whether the American Association of Neurology [sic] guidelines are considered "accepted medical standards" that satisfy the definition of brain death in NRS 451.007. We conclude that the district court failed to properly consider whether the American Association of Neurology [sic] guidelines adequately measure all functions of the entire brain, including the brain stem under NRS 451.007 and are considered accepted medical standards by states that have adopted the Uniform Determination of Death Act.[124]

The court reversed the lower court's order and placed a temporary restraining order on the hospital. Hailu's family moved to Reno, Nevada, to be near her as she lay in hospital, while her father battled the hospital in Nevada's courts. Hailu died of respiratory failure on January 4, 2016.

Hailu's case represented a serious legal challenge that questioned whether current medical guidelines for determining death comply with the UDDA and state laws that define whole brain death. While the UDDA does not identify what constitutes "accepted medical standards," and the law commissioners who drafted it were loath to step into those rough currents and prescribe the practice of medicine, the Supreme Court of Nevada correctly determined that American Academy of Neurology guidelines do not satisfy the letter of the law, because they do not determine the cessation of functions of the entire brain. The challenge brought by Hailu's family ultimately resulted in the state of Nevada changing its law in 2019, specifically to address which medical guidelines constitute accepted medical standards. The new statute retains the whole brain definition of death as irreversible cessation of "[a]ll functions of the person's entire brain, including his or her brain stem," but also endorses specific clinical guidelines that diagnose brainstem death rather than whole brain death: the guidelines by the American Academy of Neurology for adults, and the guidelines of the Pediatric Section of the Society of Critical Care Medicine, as currently promulgated, or as revised in the future.[125]

Nevada also amended the law to explicitly exempt the brain death examination from consent requirements: "A determination of the death of a person . . . is a clinical decision that does not require the consent of the person's authorized representative or the family member with the authority to consent or withhold consent."[126] The revised law also prohibits withdrawal of "organ-sustaining treatment" from a dead pregnant person with a viable fetus.

3 The Reinvention of the Person

3.1 The Metaphysics of Brain Death

A long-standing debate concerning brain death is whether it is equivalent to biological death (understood, broadly, as the point at which the organism ceases to have the characteristics of a living organism). The Harvard Ad Hoc Committee, for example, claimed equivalence by stating that the brain dies when the heart stops beating and respiration ceases. It is, of course, true that circulatory–respiratory death will eventually result in the death of the entire body, including the brain. But that fact of the matter doesn't prove equivalence so much as causation. They also claimed that the permanently nonfunctioning brain is "for all practical purposes dead."[127] That is an unproven assumption that very much depends on how we define death, and whether "for all practical purposes" death is actually death. So it doesn't follow, necessarily, that when the patient's brain is permanently nonfunctioning, the patient is dead. In 1981, the President's Commission said: "Even if life continues in individual cells or organs, life of the organism as a whole requires complex integration, and without the latter, a *person* cannot properly be regarded as alive."[128] The UK Academy doesn't try to define *biological* death, but rather the death of the *person*: "Death entails the irreversible loss of those essential characteristics which are necessary to the existence of a living human person."[129] This avoids the necessity of claiming equivalence between brain death and circulatory–respiratory death as it is traditionally understood. They are *redefining* death as, not the death of a biological organism, but the death of a *person*: "the definition of death should be regarded as the irreversible loss of the capacity for consciousness, combined with the irreversible loss of the capacity to breathe."[130] Both of these capacities are lost, as it happens, when there is damage to the brainstem, specifically damage to the reticular formation. And the relevant parts of "living human person" are obviously "living" and "person" since membership in the human species is presumably resistant to damage to the reticular formation. So, this is explicitly a definition of the death of the *person*, for which the anatomical proxy is irreversible damage to the reticular activating system. Although this is a controversial definition of death, it is a definition that is accepted by many people. It aligns with a belief, also controversial, and also acceptable to many people, that the permanent loss of consciousness is analogous to the loss or death of personhood. It aligns, then, with a higher brain definition of death (although that definition only requires the permanent loss of consciousness).The idea that the loss of consciousness is analogous to the death of the person has been a persistent theme in bioethics and medical discourses, particularly in discussions of disorders of consciousness, and the Vegetative State/Unresponsive Wakefulness Syndrome. We should be careful, however, about what we actually mean when we say that loss of consciousness is analogous to the death of personhood. Analogies are not statements of fact. Some people mean "literally dead." Some mean "as good as dead." And some mean it in a prescriptive way, and say that unconscious individuals "should be treated *as if* they are dead" (which is to say, not medically treated at all).

The most plausible justification for having a definition of brain death is that significant and devastating brain injuries resulting in the irreversible loss of consciousness result in the death of the *moral person*. But that's not a biological or medical or legal fact – biology, medicine, and the law do not tell us what moral persons are, or when they begin, and when they end. The issue we have been evading, the bush we have been beating around for decades now, is this. We are not merely harmonizing modern medicine, the law, and biological facts. We are deciding *what makes human existence valuable*, and *whose lives are valuable and worth continuing*, and imposing a particular moral viewpoint that is at odds with the metaphysics of many cultural, social, and spiritual traditions.

It is also in considerable tension with modern medicine and its endorsement of empirical, scientific, and evidence-based practice, because neurological criteria for death tacitly endorse "a metaphysical position that persons are reducible to functioning brains."[131] This is a form of metaphysical dualism in which the body and person (or consciousness, or soul) can come apart:

> The idea that persons (in the metaphysical and moral sense) can die while their physical bodies remain alive makes intuitive sense and is acceptable to many people, for many cultural and spiritual traditions contain an implicit or explicit dualism in which body and soul can part ways. But the declaration that *this moral or metaphysical person has shuffled off this mortal coil* is not a medical diagnosis nor a matter for the law.[132]

Nair-Collins argues, similarly, that metaphysical or ethical definitions of personhood are outside the scope of medicine:

> Death is a biological phenomenon, and furthermore the expertise of medicine lies in biology and related areas, not in defining the essential nature of personhood and the self. Certainly the possibility or impossibility of

preserved consciousness is ethically relevant for whether to withdraw life-sustaining treatment or allow organ procurement, but this is not the same as identifying whether the patient is already dead.[133]

The metaphysical dualism baked into brain death can transform persons into nonpersons, and it has ethical implications: It converts persons with rights, subjects of justice, into nonpersons who no longer have rights. The legal implications are similar: that former person's surrogates no longer have the right to make decisions about how or whether they are treated, and sometimes about whether or not their organs are donated.

3.2 Brain Death as a Legal Fiction

Brain death has been described as a "legal fiction."[134] Like other legal fictions, it is a legal standard that imposes a bright line on phenomena where there might be natural variation. The age of majority is one instance: Not all individuals mature at the same rate or time, nor is there a magical change that occurs in the minute that passes between when an adolescent is 17 and when they turn 18, but it is legally useful to determine an arbitrary point at which a person can be considered an adult, rather than try to determine capacities on a case by case basis. "Legal fictions serve a very legitimate role in society, by facilitating important social functions, particularly in situations where the necessary function may not entirely conform to the material facts."[135] Shah has defined brain death specifically as a "status legal fiction," one that changes the status of a human being from living to dead, and allows us to treat that individual as if they are dead.

> A legal fiction is a somewhat counterintuitive device that relies on falsehoods to extend the law into new areas. Legal fictions arise when the law treats something that is false (or not known to be true) as if it were actually true.[136]
>
> A status legal fiction is an analogy in which one entity is treated as if it has the status of a different type of entity for the purpose of applying an existing legal framework.[137]

Shah argues that the law should "pierce the veil" of brain death, and should not use this legal fiction in cases where there are objections to brain death that are based on religious and moral objections.[138] The lack of transparency about brain death as a legal fiction, she argues, makes whole brain death "an especially dangerous type of legal fiction since it is opaque and unacknowledged, and therefore vulnerable to misuse."[139]

Reflecting on Jahi McMath, Shah notes that the family's distrust of the medical team was likely exacerbated by the insistence on brain death as legal death and as reality:

Having a physician state unequivocally that someone who is brain dead is dead, despite displaying visible signs associated with life, is incredibly hard to believe. For those who already lack trust in their physicians, the claims are possibly even harder to believe. In the McMath case, the family did not appear to believe that Jahi McMath had permanently lost her ability to interact with the world in a meaningful way.

The McMath family might have had reasons to seek continued care for Jahi. First, if the family had strong views that all life is sacred and was willing to pay or obtain financing for Jahi's care to keep her alive, their deeply held beliefs might have motivated their decision.[140]

Jahi McMath's case exemplifies the way that brain death as a legal fiction can promote discord. In the state of California, Jahi had been declared brain dead, and was considered legally dead. In the state of New Jersey, she was considered alive, medically, socially, and legally, and retained her legal rights as a person. Those rights included the right of her parents to make medical decisions on her behalf. The difference was not one of biology, or even brain function, but of geopolitical location, and social/cultural/religious differences in the populations of the two states. Thus, the legal status of brain death doesn't track biological facts so much as sociopolitical and legal ones, notwithstanding decades of effort to defend its equivalency to biological death.

Not all legal fictions are benign or protective, and some, like the status legal fiction of brain death, do not extend rights (as the fiction of the age of adulthood does), but rather function to obliterate rights, by severing the individual from the community of legal and moral persons. Brain death as a legal fiction intrudes on significant social, cultural, spiritual, and personal aspects of human life. It diminishes the moral and legal rights of the individual determined to be dead; it severs important social connections and relationships; and it precipitates a host of important and irrevocable social and legal practices.

It cannot be denied that death is important. It's important personally, spiritually, and socially. It marks the end of a person's existence. As a practical matter, the absence of a universal, culturally accepted understanding of death "can lead to distress and conflict when local, accepted medical practice clashes with cultural and religious tenets."[141] As Shah argues, brain death as a legal fiction was not the product of democratic deliberation, and "[g]iven the relatively shaky democratic foundations of the legal fiction of brain death, accommodation of opposing views about death seems especially warranted here."[142]

3.3 A Matter of Justice

Brain death raises issues of justice, not least because it is burdensome only for those who object to neurological criteria for death. Laws have coercive force, and medical guidelines and hospital policies trade on the power of legal death statutes to unliterally make decisions. That coercive force is specifically brought to bear on those who object to brain death, who are subjected to involuntary and unilateral withdrawal of life-sustaining treatment, and even organ procurement. In other words, the impact of brain death is not equal for all patients and their families. As a legal fiction, brain death transforms a living person into a corpse, and strips away their legal rights. It also takes from families and surrogates their rights to make decisions on behalf of the patient. The burdens associated with brain death are "neither benign nor equally distributed, and are thus unjust."[143]

Truog points to factors that contribute to family objections to a diagnosis of brain death:

> [A] dominant factor driving these refusals is family mistrust in the healthcare providers. Not surprisingly, race, ethnicity, and socioeconomic status were associated with refusals, undoubtedly aggravated by the high rates of discordance by race and religiosity between the physicians and the families.[144]

Paquette et al. studied the reasons behind family objections, and found many that were related to race and ethnicity, socioeconomic status, and membership in disadvantaged groups:

> Several reasons for objecting to DNC were associated with groups already disadvantaged in medicine (15). Race and ethnicity were associated with needing time for others to arrive. Ethnicity was associated with prior trauma and language barriers. Those of lower [socioeconomic status] were more likely not to want to "give up." Those with lower educational attainment were more likely to hold misinformed beliefs that individuals could "wake up" after declaration of DNC. Those who had experienced mistrust were more likely to want not to give up, wait on a miracle or not believe in DNC.[145]

Families that object to determinations of neurological death sometimes express religious or cultural objections, while others express "concerns about a rush to judgment, perceptions of negligent or indifferent treatment of their loved ones, and fears about the exploitation of organ donors," all of which point to mistrust in medical providers and systems.[146] Jahi McMath's family expressed concerns about the lack of compassion they received from medical staff, their mistrust in the hospital and staff, and suspicions that their mistreatment was racially motivated. Interpersonal factors and conflicts are always possible in circumstances in which patients, families, and healthcare staff have differing views about medical treatment, but "the legacy of distrust of medical providers among historically marginalized and exploited communities cannot be discounted as a factor."[147] The experiences of families like

Jahi McMath's must be viewed in the context of a long history of discrimination and racial disparities in access to healthcare and in objective health outcomes that continues to affect marginalized and racialized communities today, and is experienced worldwide by minority and immigrant communities as well.[148] There are also well-documented intergroup differences concerning end-of-life preferences and preferences concerning the withdrawal of life-sustaining treatment.[149] When those differences are ignored by institutional policies for managing so-called futile treatment or brain death determinations, those one-size-fits-all policies "can target and burden marginalized and vulnerable patients and their families in their implementation, if not their intention."[150] The medicolegal determination of brain death is coercive in a way that is irrevocable, and not equally distributed:

> The coercive force of laws, policies, and guidelines is specifically brought to bear on those who resist death by neurologic criteria, and not on those who accept it. In practice, they treat alike only those who agree that death by neurologic criteria is death. Those who deny that it is death are likely to be subjected to the involuntary withdrawal of life-sustaining treatment and, in some cases, procurement of organs against the wishes of the family or surrogate.[151]

Indeed, the intention of enacting policies may be benign, and may well be motivated by concerns about preventing bias and unequal treatment. I have argued that

> when racial, ethnic, cultural, and religious minorities are harmed more frequently and disproportionately by policies implemented on the bodies of their children and loved ones, those policies do not effectively prevent bias and are not neutral. Moreover, the *appearance of bias*, particularly concerning a matter as emotional and culturally laden with meaning and import as death, further erodes trust in persons and communities that already have reasons to be distrustful of healthcare providers.[152]

The effects of a determination of brain death for the person declared dead and their family are particularly and uniquely onerous. It is argued that brain death is death because it is the death of the person.[153] But here, too, brain death involves a self-fulfilling prophecy, for the death of the person as a subject of morality, as a subject of rights and justice, as a member of the moral, legal, and social communities, follows from the declaration of brain death. These many "deaths," of course, are also experienced in death according to circulatory–respiratory criteria, but there, the presumed death of the person does not precede or determine their moral, social, and legal death, but rather occurs simultaneously with their biological death.

3.4 The Dead Donor Rule and Organ Donation

There is controversy about whether DCD violates the Dead Donor Rule, an informal ethical rule that requires that organ donors are dead before their organs are procured. The rule is intended to safeguard the organ donor against being killed by removal of their organs. Some have argued that DCD donors are dead when their organs are procured; others have argued they are not.[154] Arguably, DCD donors are *dying*, but until their hearts have ceased beating beyond the possibility of autoresuscitation, they are not yet dead.[155] An additional wrinkle for adherence to the Dead Donor Rule is the controversial DCD practice of normothermic regional perfusion, which uses ECMO to restore circulation to the abdominal organs of the donor, which would seemingly reverse circulatory arrest and death, while the blood flow to the brain is clamped off, which would seemingly induce anoxic brain death.[156] It has, of course, also been said of those determined to be *brain* dead that their functioning bodies preclude their being dead, although in many cases, they are dying, or will soon (after life-sustaining treatment is withdrawn) certainly be dead. Both the brain dead and those dead by circulatory–respiratory criteria can be organ donors on the assumption that the Dead Donor Rule is not violated.

Questions about whether current determinations of whole brain death satisfy the definition of whole brain death – if the hypothalamus or pituitary gland continue to function, if there is isolated electrical activity, or if there is global ischemic penumbra – thus raise further questions about whether the Dead Donor Rule is violated when individuals determined to be dead by neurological criteria have their organs removed for donation.

Truog and Miller argue that adherence to the Dead Donor Rule has forced "unnecessary and unsupportable revisions of the definition of death" to accommodate organ donation, and "[a]t worst, this ongoing reliance suggests that the medical profession has been gerrymandering the definition of death to carefully conform with conditions that are most favorable for transplantation."[157] They have argued that the Dead Donor Rule also thwarts those who might want to be organ donors, but who are not eligible under current definitions of death, and results in valuable organs being lost to ischemia during DCD protocols.

It has always been the case that the need for viable, life-saving organs for transplantation has motivated and animated efforts to redefine death, and the Dead Donor Rule has functioned as a backstop to prevent, as it were, a slide down a slippery slope to medical homicide. It is equally the case that gerrymandering death solely to meet the needs of organ transplant recipients risks exploiting individuals with brain injuries, and sacrificing them for the sake of others. Much hinges, then, on both how death is defined and how it is determined for purposes of organ donation.

3.5 Case Study: Elijah Smith

Elijah Smith was 21 years old when he was struck by a car while riding his bicycle in Columbus, Ohio, United States. The year before, he had indicated his willingness to be an organ donor on his driver's license. Lifeline of Ohio, the organ procurement organization, was notified by Grant Medical Center of Smith's status as a donor and he was declared brain dead. His parents, Pamela and Rodney Smith, indicated that they did not consent to donation of Smith's organs because he did not understand the choice he was making when he agreed to donation. Specifically, they did not think their son understood that his heart would still be beating when his organs were removed for donation. "We do not want our son to die like this. We do not want our son to be an organ donor," Smith's mother said.[158] Pamela Smith stated that she believed death occurred when all organs ceased functioning. She said "We wanted for him to be unplugged, to see him die completely, so that we could accept that we did everything we could. We were still hoping against hope that he would breathe. We knew that wasn't very likely."[159]

Under Ohio law, only a potential organ donor can revoke or amend their organ donor status. Lifeline sought a court order to obtain Smith's organs over the objections of his parents, stating: "We are obligated and responsible for fulfilling that wish to be a donor." The court sided with Lifeline, and Elijah Smith's organs were procured for transplantation. Smith's mother said that Lifeline had "gone behind our backs ... to get my son's organs."[160]

Smith's parents expressed a view that is not uncommon among families who dispute a brain death determination, that the declaration of death is a pretext for an "organ grab." In a California case, Michael O'Connor sued Fresno Community Hospital and Donor Network West, the organ procurement organization, for intentional infliction of emotional distress by engaging in subterfuge to obtain his 26-year-old daughter's organs. O'Connor's lawyers describe the organ procurement organization as "overzealous" and accuses them of "manipulative bad faith behavior, which reflects a widespread problem in the organ procurement 'industry'."[161] The family of Gregory Jacobs, an 18-year-old in Pennsylvania who sustained a brain injury while snowboarding, sued for wrongful death and claimed he was "intentionally killed at Hamot Hospital so that his organs could be harvested."[162]

Circulatory–respiratory death more closely matches most people's intuitions about what constitutes death than does brain death, in which the heart continues to beat and the patient breathes, albeit with a ventilator. It's unclear how well the individuals asked to donate their organs understand how their death will be determined in the event they are candidates for donation. In a review of empirical data on public understanding of brain death, Shah et al. conclude that "despite scholarly claims of widespread public support for organ donation from brain dead patients, the existing, geographically diverse data on public attitudes regarding brain death and organ transplantation reflect substantial public confusion."[163] Their review found a widespread lack of understanding about organ donation and brain death:

> The empirical literature demonstrates that both members of the general public and family members who have made decisions about organ donation often do not understand three key issues: (1) uncontested biological facts about the condition of patients meeting the clinical criteria for a diagnosis of brain death, (2) that organs can legally be procured from patients who have been determined to be brain dead and (3) that organs are procured from brain dead patients while their hearts are still beating and before they are disconnected from ventilators.[164]

Widespread confusion about brain death or the determination of death prior to organ donation have a number of potentially negative consequences. Elijah Smith's parents claimed that he did not understand what he was agreeing to when he agreed to be an organ donor. It is likely that many people do not understand that their hearts will be beating when their organs are removed for donation and transplantation following brain death. Brain death is deeply counterintuitive, and rarely encountered by most people. After all, brain death accounts for only a small percentage of hospital deaths. The circumstances under which people are asked to be donors – in the United States, it is frequently when they apply for a driver's license or state-issued identification card – are by no stretch of the imagination circumstances that can come close to those that would be adequate for informed consent in medical contexts. Potential donors have no opportunity to obtain information or education about what it means to agree to donation. Furthermore, potential donors may not be aware that some states – like Ohio – do not permit the patient's surrogates or family members to object to organ donation.

In a 2019 study of Americans, the *National Survey of Organ Donation Attitudes and Practices*, the majority of respondents support organ donation (90.4 percent) and believe it to be beneficial. But those numbers have decreased since the last survey, in 2012. In all, 42.1 percent of respondents believe that it's possible for a brain-dead patient to recover, and that belief is highest among Black and Asian respondents (51 percent and 49.8 percent, respectively). The number of respondents who think that the system is unfair to minorities, and that they are less likely to receive organs, has risen sharply, to 48 percent (compared to 29 percent in 2005 and 30 percent in 2012). And only about half of those Americans who support organ donation have registered as donors.[165]

One potential consequence of the lack of information and transparency about organ donation practices is that the agreement of potential donors is not sufficiently informed, which gives us reason to question its validity. As Shah et al. point out, public confusion could also "compromise the validity of any conclusions that the public supports our current practices regarding organ [donation after brain death]."[166] A serious consequence is that individuals faced with decisions concerning donation, as well as communities and publics, will lack trust in the medical practices for determining death, the medical practitioners involved in those death determinations, and the organ procurement and donation systems. The National Survey shows that trust in organ donation has diminished sharply in the United States over the years, with 31.9 percent of respondents agreeing that doctors are *less* likely to save donors (compared to 16 percent in 2005 and 20 percent in 2012). Among Black respondents, that number rose to 42.6 percent.[167] That lack of trust may lead some to believe, as Elijah Smith's and Gregory Jacobs' families, and Brittany O'Connor's father, that they or their loved ones might be intentionally killed for their organs.

4 Social, Cultural, and Spiritual Objections to Brain Death

4.1 A Problem for Technologically and Medically Advanced Societies

Brain death is rare. It accounts for only 1–2 percent of hospital deaths in the United States and the 2–3 percent in the European Union.[168] Brain injuries of various etiologies can lead to brain death: traumatic brain injuries, brain hemorrhages, anoxic and hypoxic brain injuries resulting from cardiac arrests and drowning, and so on. Some brain injuries are so immediately catastrophic that patients cannot be stabilized or kept alive long enough for a brain death determination (or, for that matter, for hospitalization). For others, regardless of the cause of the brain injury, the pathophysiological process that leads to brain death is the same: a cascade of edema (brain swelling), which increases intracranial pressure (i.e., pressure that builds in the brain because it is encased in an inflexible skull), which decreases cerebral blood flow and perfusion, and eventual brain herniation, leading to complete cessation of blood flow. For Jahi

McMath, uncontrolled postsurgical bleeding that led to a prolonged cardiac arrest was the precipitating cause of her hypoxic brain injury, but edema precipitated the diagnosis of brain death.

As a medical, legal, social, and ethical problem, brain death is a problem that only exists where the intensive medical technology is available to maintain life in patients with brain injuries who are comatose. Outside of those settings, the injuries that could lead to brain death are often swiftly fatal.

For reasons rooted in traditional, cultural, and religious beliefs, not all technologically and medically advanced societies have an accepted or legally and medically endorsed definition of brain death. In Japan and South Korea, for example, brain death exists solely to facilitate organ transplantation, and family consent is required for both transplantation and the determination of death; in China, brain death determination protocols exist, but there is no law concerning brain death. Terunuma and Mathis describe "the crux of the brain death issue in Asia" as that "Western medicine, which itself has not fully decided on brain death, has issued guidelines taught to Asian doctors that conflict with traditional views of life, illness, medical care, death, and families that have been cemented into Confucian traditions."[169] Similarly, India defines brain death only in the context of organ donation, and patients whose families refuse consent for donation continue to receive medical treatment until circulatory–respiratory death because "there are no guidelines about disconnecting the ventilator in a situation when organ donation is not authorised by the family."[170]

The societies in which brain deaths occur, and in which they can be controversial, are not cultural or social monoliths. Like the United States and the United Kingdom, they can be multicultural and pluralistic, with people from diverse social, cultural, and ethnic backgrounds, and diverse religious and spiritual traditions and communities. Those are settings in which conflicts can arise between the metaphysical worldview that is accepted in medicine and the law, and the worldviews endorsed by diverse publics.

4.2 Conscience and Accommodation

There is a need to know who has died and when they have died. The answers to these important questions have long been societally and culturally defined, but "death became more complex and fit less easily into traditional understandings as a result of medical interventions."[171] The importance of death provides a reason for the law and medical practice to accommodate important and reasonable conscientious objections to brain death, for the legal fiction of brain death should "not be brandished to instrumentalize persons, to treat them as organ donors who exist only to serve others, or as corpses to whom we owe nothing."[172] As I have argued elsewhere, "[t]here is a decided lack of consensus concerning the definition of death, but it is certain that objections to whole-brain death can be based on genuine, deeply held, and deeply important moral and/or religious convictions. There is an evident need for tolerance and accommodation of such conscientious objections to declarations of death by neurological criteria."[173]

Death by circulatory–respiratory criteria is nearly universally accepted as death across individuals, societies, cultures, spiritual traditions, nations, and in the law. Some societies accept only circulatory–respiratory criteria for death. In countries like the United States and the United Kingdom, circulatory–respiratory and neurological criteria for death exist and are medically and legally endorsed. In Canada, although a single definition of death – brainstem death – is now medically endorsed, there are still circulatory–respiratory criteria for determining brain death (although whether this clarifies or muddies the waters remains to be seen). There are compelling reasons to permit sincere, conscientious objections to brain death given the medical, ethical, legal, spiritual, cultural, and philosophical (epistemic and metaphysical) challenges to brain death. Circulatory–respiratory criteria for death are globally endorsed and are an acceptable alternative to those who object to neurological criteria, and it is both reasonable and feasible to accommodate conscientious objections –as exemplified in the law that exists in New Jersey in the United States – that accept circulatory–respiratory death as an alternative to brain death. Indeed, an additional practical reason to do so is that it permits transparency about the status of brain death as a legal fiction – and for many people, devastating brain injuries are "close enough" to count as death. It might also make less important the academic/medical/philosophical debate about the appropriate criteria for death, and neurological death in particular, to the extent that it would matter less how brain death is diagnosed if those who object to the diagnosis are informed and have the opportunity to "opt out." There are numerous reasons to permit conscientious objections:

> Allowing individuals and their surrogates to choose continuation or withdrawal of treatment and choose the death that aligns with reasonable, medically and socially accepted beliefs also aligns with core ethical values in medicine, including respecting persons and respecting patient and surrogate autonomy. It answers the demands of justice. It fosters trust and patient-centered care, and treats grieving and struggling families with compassion as they make the most weighty, consequential, highly emotional, and momentous decisions many will ever face.[174]

Veatch has argued that public policy should accommodate reasonable consciences and basic beliefs about human existence and death, including whole brain or brainstem death, higher brain death, and circulatory–respiratory (or somatic) death, and the variants within them:

> What is at stake is fundamental to human existence: the right of individuals to hold basic beliefs about what it is about life that is so important that its loss is taken as evidence that someone is no longer with us as a member of the human moral community. Respecting the right of individuals to make choices within reason about what it means to die is so critical that we must be willing to tolerate the difficulties that might arise as a result. It seems likely that those difficulties will be minimal and the gains enormous.[175]

Veatch and Ross have similarly argued for a "conscience clause" that permits competent individuals to choose an alternative definition of death (so long as it is within reason and poses no public health risks), noting that "there is no consensus on the definition of death."[176]

4.3 Case Study: Child A

On February 6, 2015, in Manchester, England, a 19-month-old boy who came to be known in court documents as Child A choked on a small piece of fruit and fell unconscious. His mother immediately called for an ambulance, and Child A was ventilated en route to Central Manchester University Hospital. He was in respiratory distress when he arrived, and within half an hour had suffered a cardiac arrest. About 20 minutes later, his cardiac function was restored. Child A was intubated, and the bit of fruit, a satsuma, was removed. The pediatric intensive care unit administered neuroprotective measures.

The following day, an MRI scan was performed, which showed, according to the High Court decision, "extensive severe ischemic changes involving the grey matter of Child A's brain."[177] On February 10, two brainstem death examinations were performed at 10:10 am and 5:30 pm, and both confirmed brainstem death. Child A had symptoms of cardiovascular instability and diabetes insipidus. Child A's parents, Muslims and Saudi citizens, sought to take their son home to Saudi Arabia to continue medical treatment. Justice Hayden of the UK High Court Family Division describes the family's pain, and their motives:

> In my view, it is almost impossible for any adult to absorb the extent of the parent's distress. Human instinct senses that level of pain and recoils from it. Ultimately, all we, the lawyers and doctors, can do is to offer Mr and Mrs A and their family our profound sympathies and condolence. This is a Muslim family. Mr A has wanted to cleave to what thread of life he perceives his son still to have.

I was not at all surprised to hear from him, in evidence, that his real
motivation was to take Child A to Saudi Arabia in the hope that he might live.
In Saudi Arabia, the father told me, for religious reasons, a life support
machine would never be switched off.[178]

The family disagreed with the determination of brainstem death, and Child
A remained on ventilatory and medical support. A strange turn of events then
put the matter before the UK High Court Family Division. The senior coroner
became aware of the child, and asserted jurisdiction over his "body," writing to
the hospital director:

> *Technically, I have assumed jurisdiction over the body. It seems wholly
> inappropriate for a deceased body to be intubated and ventilated when this
> is futile and, to my mind, unethical. Accordingly, I must ask you to cease this
> and extubate him so that his body can be moved to the mortuary from which it
> can be released to his parents. If the family wish to repatriate his body to
> Saudi Arabia, then I will provide an out of England certificate. Obviously,
> your clinicians will need to communicate this to the parents and allow a short
> but reasonable time for the parents to be with him pending the extubation.*
> [italics in original][179]

Interestingly, Justice Hayden appeared to scold the coroner in his ruling, noting
that he "might well reflect now whether that kind of language was suitable in
such sensitive circumstances,"[180] and stated: "I cannot conceive of any circumstances in which the Coroner should seek to intervene, where a body remains
ventilated, beyond those circumstances concerning the removal of organs where
the family are consenting. Any other approach I regard as likely to generate
immense distress and contribute to an atmosphere where sound judgment may
be jeopardised."[181]

The hospital sought a court ruling to resolve the matter and grant permission
to withdraw ventilatory support without the parents' consent. The court, despite
stating that "in a multi-cultural society there has to be recognition that people,
particularly those with strong religious beliefs, may differ with medical profes-
sionals as to when death occurs," ruled that Child A was dead and that treatment
should be ceased: "Whilst expressing profound respect for the father's views,
the time has now come to permit the ventilator to be turned off and to allow
Child A, who died on 10th February, dignity in death."[182]

Brierly reports that the case marked the first "legal acceptance of brainstem death as equating to death of the person" in the United Kingdom, noting
the lack of a legal definition of death in UK law.[183] The UK Parliament has
not enacted laws regarding brainstem death or the withdrawal of life support,
so conflicts over brain death have continued to be resolved in the courts, and
the courts have subsequently upheld the legality of brainstem death in

several cases.[184] These include another case involving a Muslim family at the very same hospital, Manchester University Hospital, where Child A died. Midrar Namiq was declared brainstem dead two weeks after a complicated birth: A cord prolapse deprived him of oxygen while his mother was en route to the hospital. His parents said that their imam advised them not to agree to a withdrawal of ventilation. The judge ruled that when brain death criteria are met, "the patient has irreversibly lost whatever one might define as life," and granted the hospital's request for a declaration that it would be lawful to withdraw ventilation, to allow "a kind and dignified death" for the baby.[185]

Choong and Rady argue that Child A was not dead according to the religious beliefs of his parents:

> The delay in withdrawing mechanical ventilation was precipitated by Child A's parents' refusal to accept brainstem death as synonymous with death in the Islamic faith. The signs that distinguish between life and death are well-described in the Islamic scriptures. From a religious viewpoint, death is demarcated by the soul's departure from the body. The soul's presence is associated with the continuation of a beating heart and the perpetuation of breathing, even if aided by artificial ventilation, as was the case with Child A; consequently, this person is still considered alive.[186]

Choong and Rady conclude that "the legal system in the United Kingdom should not favour a secular definition of death over a definition of death that is respectful of religious values about the inviolability and sanctity of life."[187] They further recommend that "the British judiciary and/or legislators accommodate and respect residents' religious rights and commitments when secular conceptions of death based on medical codes and practices conflict with a traditional concept well-grounded in religious and cultural values and practices. Respecting cultural values and religious beliefs strengthens the protection of human rights in a multicultural society."[188]

Donnelly and Lyons observe that, in the absence of a statutory scheme, "DNC in the UK continues to be grounded in the common law,"[189] and one outcome of the increasing number of family challenges to brain death determinations is "an ad hoc form of 'reasonable accommodation' of alternative views of DNC."[190] The accommodations the courts have granted have been limited, however. "There is also a lack of clarity as regards what a court might do in terms of reasonable accommodation. To date, the accommodation afforded by the UK courts has been allowing families time to say goodbye before removal of somatic support."[191] While more time is something many families desire when facing the imminent death of a loved one, it is a far cry from what the parents of Child A and Midrar Namiq were seeking: They sought continuation of life support and the transfer of their children. If Child A's parents had succeeded in repatriating their son back to their homeland, it is not clear why they should have been stopped from doing so, or what business it was of a UK court or hospital whether they did. Equally unclear is why withdrawing life support from their young son was a better alternative – notwithstanding the court's claim that it allowed him "dignity in death" (which is of questionable value to a toddler) – than allowing him to leave the hospital and the country to continue treatment in Saudi Arabia.

5 Is There an End in Sight?

5.1 Death Is Different

Death comes for us all, across humanity, across species. In that sense, it is nothing special, just the ending of every living organism's physical existence. Even seemingly immortal and indestructible creatures like tardigrades and immortal jellyfish die. Similarly, humans are not alone in attaching importance to death, in performing rituals that acknowledge the dead, and grieving their dead.[192] Indeed, humans also grieve the loss of the animals with whom they share their lives.[193] Death is universally experienced by every person, either as their own death or as the deaths of others, and for most of us, both.

And yet, death is undoubtedly special as a human experience, for it marks not only the end of a living organism, or a mortal body, but also of a *person*, a locus of emotional attachment, an entity of moral concern, someone situated in the world of a family and a community. Sometimes that end is untimely, as when a child dies. Sometimes, it is less so, the inevitable ending to a long life well-lived. Sometimes, for many reasons, a death can be hard to accept because it disrupts the natural order of things – the loss of a child does this. Sometimes a death is hard to accept because it is unexpected.

And sometimes, as in cases of brain death, it is hard to accept because it is out of alignment with deeply rooted cultural, spiritual, personal, or philosophical understandings about what death is and what it looks like. Because the brain-dead body is warm to the touch, and has a beating heart and coursing blood, and a chest rising and falling with every breath. The body's wounds heal, the limbs twitch. To call such a body a *cadaver* or a *corpse* is, seemingly, to gravely misunderstand what those words mean. To issue a death certificate seems a wild mistake. For a coroner to assert jurisdictional authority over the body seems an impudent blunder.

In describing Child A's parents, Justice Hayden seemingly attributes their refusal to remove life support to grief, rather than to their religious or cultural beliefs about life and death: "Child A's parents have simply been unable to contemplate turning off ventilatory support. Mr A clings on to any sign that may undermine these catastrophic medical conclusions, pointing to the twitching and retraction of Child A's legs, which are spinal, not cerebral reactions. That seems to me to be entirely understandable."[194]

Grief is not to be dismissed – it is an appropriate, expected response to the death of a loved one. Yet, as an emotion, an especially powerful one at that, we might be tempted to think it obliterates the rational, makes it impossible for the grieving parent to "see" what is before their eyes and evident to doctors, to "understand" or "contemplate" – to think rationally about – the fact that the child before them, with a beating heart, is dead. We might be tempted to think that grief alone explains why some families reject the notion of brain death and reject the very idea that their beloved child, or mother, or brother, is dead. But, of course, people in the grip of potent grief understand, every day, everywhere in the world, that someone they care about has died. Brain death is deeply counterintuitive to those who haven't drunk the Kool-Aid, and it does not align with the worldviews, the cultural, spiritual, and metaphysical beliefs of many people around the world. It is, in a very real sense, a modern invention, a solution to problems created by medical innovations and interventions, and modern impatience with deaths that, because we have intervened, inconveniently do not arrive on time. But they are also deaths that defy expectations about death, and so look like premature declarations of death when a person is mostly dead, but still slightly alive.

5.2 Are There Truly Dead Brains?

In the beginning, the Harvard Committee asserted that the permanently non-functioning brain is "for all practical purposes dead."[195] The Harvard diagnostic criteria included coma, no movement or breathing, absent reflexes, and a "flat or isoelectric EEG."[196] The technology of the time did not allow for testing of cerebral perfusion, the loss or impairment of which precipitates neurological death. These criteria shaped the definition of whole brain death, but the neurological determination of whole brain death has evolved in the decades since. As already discussed, the American Academy of Neurology clinical guidelines currently in wide use exclude evidence that some parts of the brain, like the hypothalamus and pituitary gland, are functioning, and also do not require a flat EEG – some electrical activity in the brain is compatible with current guidelines for determining whole brain death. The UK and Canadian guidelines for brainstem death are even more stripped down, and call for irreversible (in the United Kingdom) or permanent (in Canada) loss of the capacity for consciousness and the capacity to breathe. In practice, the tests used to diagnose whole brain and brainstem death are the same – they test for brainstem-mediated reflexes (not, as in the Harvard criteria, *all* reflexes), apnea, and unconsciousness.

What would it take for an entire brain to be truly, functionally dead? The Harvard criteria come close, although they also effectively rule out the presence of spinal reflexes (like the Lazarus sign). It would also require the loss of perfusion and oxygenation to the brain, as that would result in the destruction and eventual necrosis of the entire brain. A number of ancillary tests are available to visualize the loss of perfusion, including single-photon emission computed tomography and positron emission tomography.[197] As Shewmon and Coimbra have pointed out, however, global ischemic penumbra is a confounder because the tests currently lack the sensitivity to completely rule out very low levels of cerebral perfusion that are compatible with cellular preservation and the prevention of necrosis.[198] There are known cases of misdiagnosis following cerebral perfusion imaging that indicate that it is not currently sufficient, although potentially repeated imaging over time might be adequately confirmatory.[199] Furthermore, Shewmon has documented long-term survivals of brain-dead individuals with significant brain necrosis, including a child who lived for three decades following diagnosis, with little brain remaining by the time he died.[200]

Diagnosing irreversible whole brain death is a significant epistemic challenge. Irreversibility is prognostic, it makes a prediction about the impossibility of recovery or reversal of the loss of brain function. In fact, it cannot be diagnosed with the kind of certainty one would ethically want when determining that someone is dead. Death is final, irreversible, and not something one recovers from. The diagnosis of brain death, as a predictive inference, cannot be certain, although it can be probable (to a greater or lesser degree). This is not a problem exclusive to the diagnosis of brain death, but one general across medicine, and especially in the context of brain injuries.[201] The extraordinary case of Jahi McMath provides evidence that our current standards are not adequate to determine irreversibility, if it is true that she recovered consciousness, and that her brain did not deteriorate in the four years after she was declared dead. Time, waiting, might have changed Jahi's diagnosis and prognosis. In the pathological cascade of cerebral edema and brain herniation, there is a point of no return, after which the destruction of the brain is complete, and necrosis will follow. Our haste in diagnosing brain death, however, puts that point beyond our knowing, and beyond our willingness to wait for more prognostic certainty. One of the factors putting time pressure on determinations of brain death is the possibility of using the organs of the dead to save the lives of others through transplantation. Another is the pressure to use limited medical resources for other patients, those we think we are able to help.

5.3 Is Brain Death Close Enough?

Many people would agree that if they should suffer a brain injury so severe that they are unlikely to ever recover consciousness, or recover the ability to do the things they care about, the things that give their lives meaning and allow them to flourish, then they might as well be dead. Others would disagree, and would hang on to life – any life – for as long as possible. What would be unendurable or unimaginable to one would be good enough for another. Neither sentiment is wrong, for what matters to individuals, what makes their lives go well or ill, involves value judgments that are deeply subjective. And fundamentally, the questions and disputes concerning brain death are questions and disputes about the meaning and importance of life, about what makes a human life worth living, and about what we ought to do when medicine has reached the limits of its ability to change the course of disease or injury, or reverse impending death.

For many people, including many doctors, brain death, however imprecise it might be, however approximate, and however uncertain, is close enough. It is death "for all practical purposes," and something not to be lived through. However much one might question whether they got the answer right, the UK Academy got the questions right: *Who is a living person?*, and *When does personhood end?* are deeply important and consequential questions. The Academy's answer, that a person ceases to exist when there is irreversible loss of the capacity for consciousness and the capacity to breathe, is a seemingly plausible answer that many would endorse.

Among the general public, there is uncertainty and doubt about brain death. Siminoff et al. found that only 40.3 percent of people think those declared brain dead are actually dead. More believe them to be "as good as dead," but not really dead.[202] When detailed information about brain-dead patients is provided – such as that the hearts of the brain dead continue to beat – the public is less likely to think brain death is death.[203] This uncertainty and confusion, as Shah has argued, the lack of transparency about brain death, and its shaky democratic foundations as a legal fiction provide reasons to be more accommodating of opposition to it.[204]

One obstacle to transparency, accommodation, and acceptance is that brain death has been framed – as a legal or medical matter – not as a subjective answer to a subjective question, but rather as an objective truth about life and death. And that does not ring true for all, nor does it align with the worldviews, the spiritual, cultural, and personal beliefs of many people. Someone who endorses some form of dualism, and further endorses that the "seat of the soul" (as Descartes would have it), or consciousness, or identity is located somewhere in the physical brain, might well accept that the destruction of the brain (or part of it) entails the loss of the soul or of personal identity or of moral and legal personhood. Yet, others who believe that death occurs when the soul departs the body accept that the breathing body is still ensouled. These are matters of belief. So are medicolegal assertions that brain death is death, for the determination of DNC would have us believe that the absence of some (important) brain functions is the equivalent of death as everyone (or nearly everyone) has always understood it. The end of a human being. The end of a moral and legal person, notwithstanding that the body in front of us that does not look or behave like a corpse, and does not look like someone who should be sent to the coroner, or put in a box to be buried, or cremated.

Neither can one simply assert scientific facts – or legal fictions – to resolve the matter for unbelievers. While the belief that death occurs when the heart stops beating and breathing ceases is, perhaps, pre-scientific, it is not wrong. Everyone accepts circulatory–respiratory criteria for death (with, perhaps, some interpretive complications for some spiritual traditions, like Buddhism), and circulatory–respiratory death is the familiar way to think about death, and to know that someone is dead. Brain death was invented because medical technology developed to reverse (often, not always) circulatory–respiratory death, and did so well enough that it forced us to question whether we had saved lives that were, for those saved, worth living. But the answer to that question is not to simply assert that those lives are not worth living because those patients are in *fact* already dead. That negates the question altogether. The answer is far more complex, and depends on social, cultural, and individual value judgments about which lives are worth *living*, and which are not. Medicine certainly accepts individual value judgments that support refusing or withdrawing medical treatment at the end of life – it does so to respect the autonomy of individual patients, and the value judgments of their surrogates. That surrogates are permitted to consent to DCD, which requires withdrawing treatment *prior* to death, in anticipation of death, is evidence of this latitude, and acceptance that individuals and their surrogates are qualified to judge whether a life will be worth living, or worth continuing. We must ask then, why that same latitude and those same value judgments are resisted when the dogma of brain death is challenged.

5.4 Can Brain Death Conflicts Be Resolved?

There are two separate arenas in which brain death is contested. Academics and scholars, philosophers, bioethicists, lawyers, physicians, and medical practitioners have been debating brain death since its invention, with no resolution in sight. They have debated its philosophical and biological rationale, the aptness and reliability of the diagnostic guidelines, issues of harm and consent, and what to do about resistance from patient families and surrogates. It's likely that patients and their families and surrogates are largely unaware of all the ink spilled in that war of words. One outcome of the publicity surrounding Jahi McMath's family's efforts to refuse withdrawal of treatment was increased public awareness that there is controversy regarding brain death. Another apparent outcome is an increase in legal challenges – on several fronts – to determinations of brain death. In the United States, this has resulted in diverse court opinions on, for example, whether the consent of a surrogate is required for the brain death examination, as well as one state, Nevada, explicitly naming the accepted medical standards that must be used.[205] (See Pope for a compendium of recent legal cases.[206]) In the United Kingdom, a similar scene has played out, with numerous legal challenges and evolving common law doctrines concerning these weighty matters, although generally speaking more deference has been given to physicians and to clinical practice guidelines in the absence of laws, and far less consideration to objections grounded in religious and cultural beliefs.[207] The United States Uniform Law Commission took up the task of revising the UDDA to bring the law into harmony with clinical practice (see note 16).

One medicolegal approach to bedside conflicts in the United States has been to use the fact of laws that define the determination of brain death to settle disputes. That is, it's possible for medical practitioners to simply assert that a patient is *legally* dead, as if that were the only matter of contention. Problematically for this approach, current clinical guidelines for diagnosing brain death are out of sync with the law, which defines brain death as the irreversible loss of *all* functions of the *entire* brain, including the brainstem. Satisfying the letter of the law is not clinically possible given the nature of the inferences and the tests involved in the diagnosis. In any case, if brain death is a *legal fiction*, then simply asserting its existence as if it represented the true nature of reality – a reality at odds with what families can see with their own eyes – will not settle the matter. Indeed, in contexts where distrust of medical practitioners is a factor, assertions of fact and invocations of the coercive force of the law are more likely to result in further breakdowns of trust and communication.

These conflicts are not impossible to resolve. A study of the frequency with which the religious exemption has been used in New Jersey, the only US state that permits opting out of brain death determinations, showed that in a five-year period, there were 30–36 exemptions statewide. The majority of hospitals surveyed reported no known requests for exemptions.[208] Brain deaths are rare, and requests for exemptions to brain death criteria for death are rarer still. It's impossible to predict how the numbers might change if exemptions and accommodations like those permitted in New Jersey were to become widely available, but one salutary effect could be that conflicts would no longer end in bruising legal and public relations battles for families and hospitals. The harms of forcing a family with a gravely injured or ill loved one into a protracted court battle are significant and many. An ethical, culturally sensitive approach is needed to resolve these conflicts in a way that respects individual autonomy, family and parental rights, diverse communities with diverse beliefs, and sound medicine. To do otherwise undermines the hard-earned but fragile trust in the medical profession, and its commitments to patient-centered care and shared decision making, because "[d]eclarations of death that do not accord with accepted cultural or spiritual understandings can appear overbearing and paternalistic to patients' families, or worse, suggest cultural imperialism, none of which are conducive to furthering understanding or compassionate care."[209]

There are important ethical reasons that argue against simply asserting that brain death is death, or that the law defines it as death. The singular importance of death calls on us to respect individual conscience while also promoting the important ethical duties of medical practitioners:

> Allowing individuals and their surrogates to choose continuation or withdrawal of treatment and choose the death that aligns with reasonable, medically and socially accepted beliefs also aligns with core ethical values in medicine, including respecting persons and respecting patient and surrogate autonomy. It answers the demands of justice. It fosters trust and patient-centered care, and treats grieving and struggling families with compassion as they make the most weighty, consequential, highly emotional, and momentous decisions many will ever face.[210]

An available approach is conveniently already baked in to existing laws and clinical guidelines that recognize that there are two ways to determine death: by neurological, and by circulatory–respiratory criteria. We might still assert, if we like (and as Canada's guidelines do), that there is but one true death, and two ways to determine it, but the important point is that rejections and refusals to recognize neurological criteria for death can be accommodated by allowing circulatory–respiratory criteria as an alternative. No one in medicine or the law denies that circulatory–respiratory death is death (although there can be questions about the precise timing of death, especially in DCD, as discussed in Section 3.4). If it is not unreasonable to accept or believe that circulatory–respiratory criteria are a valid way to determine death, we can reasonably allow conscientious refusals of brain death so long as the reasonable alternative of circulatory–respiratory death is accepted. In pluralistic, multicultural societies, there will be diverse viewpoints on contentious but deeply important and consequential matters, and "few aspects of human existence have the cultural, social, spiritual and personal gravity of death."[211] Sensitivity to cultural, spiritual, and philosophical differences in the understanding of death requires that we avoid the perception of bias, and cultural and ethical imperialism, when it comes to death, while also acknowledging that the medical understanding of death and its diagnosis is still evolving. At the policy level, permitting persons with conscientious objections to brain death to choose circulatory–respiratory death also relieves the pressure to decide, as a matter of law or policy, which definition – whole brain, brainstem, or higher brain death – is the correct one.

In the decades since the Harvard Committee took up the novel question of determining death in the irreversibly comatose, much has changed in the law and medical ethics. It is no longer "medical homicide" to withdraw medical treatment when it results in the patient's death, so long as there is consent to do so. Indeed, medical ethics, the law, and societal attitudes have evolved such that it is now common (in Western societies, and elsewhere) to withhold or withdraw treatment when the patient has indicated they do not want it, or when their surrogate has consented on their behalf. Thus, one reason for inventing brain death – to establish the permissibility of withdrawing treatment from the irreversibly comatose – is no longer needed. The other reason, to permissibly remove organs from an individual determined to be neurologically dead, remains necessary, but there too there has been medical, legal, and ethical evolution. Patients who do not satisfy brain death criteria, but whose surrogates have decided to withdraw treatment, can be eligible to donate their organs under DCD protocols (see Sections 2.1 and 3.4).

There has been another change since the Harvard Committee boldly redefined death: Neurological and intensive medical care have improved. When Beecher et al. contemplated brain death, the irreversibly comatose patients they considered could not be expected to improve, but neither was it easy to keep them alive, and all were expected to die within days or weeks due to medical instability secondary to severe brain injury. There was a case to be made that those days or weeks, followed by inevitable death, were of no value to those doomed patients. Today, we know that some patients determined to be dead according to neurological criteria can be maintained for months, and even years. There are numerous cases in the medical literature of pregnant persons kept alive for months until they gave birth to healthy infants; Jahi McMath lived for four and a half years after being declared dead. Midrar

Namiq lived for three months while his family fought the hospital in court. Indeed, his father argued that because his son had grown, and his other organs had not failed in the months since he was diagnosed as brainstem dead, he could not be dead. The justice in the case remarked on that: "In fact, it appears that Midrar may have spent the longest time in this condition of any recorded case in the UK. This means that it is unsurprising that there is no documentation on how long the heart will continue to beat in that situation, because it virtually never arises."[212] Unremarked by the justice is that the situation "virtually never arises" because in uncontested cases of brain death, life-sustaining treatment is withdrawn within hours or days. Indeed, in the contested cases, when the court rules that the patient is already dead, treatment is also withdrawn.

We also know now that brain death is sometimes misdiagnosed, even when clinical guidelines are rigorously followed.[213]

These developments should give us pause. If we maintain, as some do, that brain death amounts to the death of the person, a metaphysical and ethical entity with neurological proxies (shifting the metaphorical seat of the soul to the reticular activating system), then we might think some uncertainty is acceptable, for after all brain death is an answer to a question in the uncertain domains of ethics and metaphysics: *Who is a person?* The skeptic (or philosopher) might counter, however, that it is no business of medicine to decide the criteria for metaphysical and ethical persons – medicine's bailiwick is the physical body. Similarly, the law might legally define persons (although it rarely does), but only persons in the legal sense. The skeptic about the law's abilities there would rightly point to the frequency with which human laws have been terribly, destructively, deadly (and not so distantly) wrong about the legal personhood of, for example, Black and Indigenous persons, women, children, and disabled persons. But there are also those who assert that brain death simply tracks the nature of reality, just like circulatory–respiratory death, and that we are talking about one thing, one death, when we discuss death. Side discussions about how we determine that death, or whether it conforms to the law, while important, do not detract from the fact that brain death is death. Reality, or at least its appearance, is not on the side of that argument, and one reason is that medicine itself has changed how, when, and where we die, which is why it was necessary to reinvent death in the first place. If there is a mere "appearance" of life in those judged to be brain dead, it is an appearance propped up by the medical evidence: by the beeps and blips of heart monitors and pulse oximeters, and by the rise and fall of breathing chests as the ventilator pushes oxygen into the lungs, to be taken up by the blood that circulates through the pumping of the heart.

As an effort to practically solve a problem created by medical advancements, the invention of brain death breathed new life into ancient, deeply important, and divisive questions about life and death, and the value of human existence. It proposed that these were questions not only *posed* by modern medicine, but that could also be *answered* by modern medicine. As the intervening decades of debate have shown, the questions have become only more complex and difficult, while medicine, striving to ensure justice and compassion and scientific progress in patient care, has evolved in ways that make it less likely that the solution to the problems created by brain death – once itself the solution to problems created by medical advances – can be solved by medicine alone, or, for that matter, by legal fiat. The questions are enormously important: *What makes human existence valuable? When should a living human body be treated as a dead person?* These are fundamentally ethical and metaphysical questions for which medicine, science, and the law have no definitive answers.

5.5 Case Study: Brain Death in Japan

The history of brain death in Japan is interesting and instructive, and presents another possibility for resolving conflicts concerning the neurological determination of death.

The first heart transplant in Japan, from a brain-dead organ donor, took place in 1968. It resulted in public outcry. The transplant surgeon was accused of illegal human experimentation. In 1983, the Japanese Ministry of Health established a committee to consider brain death and transplantation, which resulted in a decades-long debate, and numerous failed attempts to pass a national law by the Diet, Japan's Parliament. In 1999, the Diet finally passed a transplantation law that recognized pluralism about death by establishing "traditional death" (or circulatory–respiratory death) and "brain death." The law requires that brain death must be chosen by an individual when they obtain an organ donor card. Brain death, in effect, only exists in Japan in the context of, and for purposes of, organ donation:

> The law states that if a person wants to be an organ donor after brain death has occurred, he or she must record that intention on a donor card or label beforehand. That person will then be considered dead when brain death is diagnosed. Those who object to brain death and transplantation do not need donor cards. They are considered to be alive until the heart stops beating. Additionally, family consent is also necessary both for legally declaring death at brain death and for organ removal. Strictly speaking, "family consent" in this law means that the family does not express objections.[214]

Japan, like other Asian countries, has several religious traditions, including the dominant religions, Buddhism and Shintoism (a polytheistic and animist religion). Terunuma and Mathis identify the Confucian roots of Japanese, Korean, and Chinese cultures as strongly influencing attitudes about the end of life and death, and impeding acceptance of brain death.

> [T]he Japanese see the mind and body as inseparable. Therefore, "brain death," or cessation of brain function independent of other body functions, is inconsistent with traditional Japanese values. For these reasons, Japanese society does not readily accept brain death. At this time, Japan (and other Asian countries) seem to be where the United States was in the 1970s and 1980s, namely grappling with medical definitions of death that are complicated by religious and cultural standards even in the face of legal definitions (again, centered around organ donation).[215]

Morioka notes that Japanese resistance to brain death is deeply rooted in their cultural and spiritual beliefs, consistent with both Buddhist and Confucian beliefs:

> The significant proportion of the Japanese people who reject the idea of brain death usually say that a brain dead patient whose body is warm and moist cannot be seen as a corpse because the essence of humans exists not only in one's mind, but also in one's body. They reject the notion that the essence of humans lies in self-consciousness and rationality. They think that a warm, living body is an integral part of the person.[216]

The traditional beliefs that ground many Asian cultures also reject the primacy of the brain and rationality, and the duality of body and soul that are common in Western belief systems.

> In Shintoism and Taoism, the native beliefs of Japan and China respectively, it is not only difficult to separate the mind from the body, human life is also intimately associated with the surrounding environment. . . . Death represents an ambiguous and gradual process with disintegration of both the physical and spiritual existences, accompanied by rituals of leave-taking and seeing-off. From the perspective of the nature worshiper, brain death is too specific and artificial.
>
> Traditional Chinese Medicine teaches that the human body is a system of correspondence, rather than a system of causation. Functions of living result from interactions between all organ systems; the brain neither controls nor integrates. In Buddhism, alaya-vijnana, or the Eighth Consciousness representing one's personal and collective identity, is distributed throughout the body and not exclusively located in the brain. Even in the absence of measurable brain activity, consciousness may still be dwelling in the body.[217]

Japan's approach to brain death requires individuals to predeclare their willingness to be determined dead by neurological criteria alongside their willingness to donate their organs, and additionally requires that their family consents to both. Only adults may self-designate as organ donors, which has made it impossible for children to be declared brain dead, or considered as organ donors, which has limited the available organs for child recipients. This is a significant downside to Japan's law, but one rooted in its culture. A simple corrective would permit families to make those decisions on behalf of their children, although this would likely be more acceptable in other societies than it would be in Japan. Morioka states that "many Japanese people think that a person's understanding of death is a very important and deeply personal thing that may be unknown even to a person's family members. This is the major argument for requiring the donor's prior declaration."[218]

Japan's law has the advantage of precluding the kinds of disputes about brain death that occur elsewhere by requiring individual and family consent, *and* by explicitly connecting brain death to organ donation. When a family rejects a declaration of brain death, they will not willingly donate the organs of their family member. In some cases, such as Elijah Smith's, organ procurement organizations in the United States will attempt to obtain the organs based solely on the prior authorization of the patient, regardless of the family's objections.

Brain death is, of course, critical to maintain the supply of much-needed organs for transplant – as was true in 1968 when brain death was proposed as a solution to ethical rules requiring that organs not be removed so as to cause death. A major practical reason for maintaining laws that recognize brain death is to facilitate legal organ procurement, yet in the United States brain death is poorly understood by Americans, and there is suspicion in some communities that the needs of organ recipients will take precedence over saving the life of a potential donor.[219] A policy like Japan's, requiring consent of the donor and their family for both a determination of neurological death and organ donation, might alleviate such concerns and avoid brain death disputes in which the family neither accepts brain death nor consents to organ donation. Whether or not one wishes to be an organ donor is already a choice in many countries, but there are reasonable doubts about whether that choice is well enough informed and understood by potential donors. The importance of brain death for organ donation ought to be openly acknowledged to inject more transparency into both organ donation and brain death. Japan's policy recognizes that there are important social, cultural, and spiritual objections to brain death as human death, and openly links individual choice concerning brain death to choice concerning organ donation and transplantation. Japan is not as early multiethnic, multicultural, and pluralistic as many other countries, such as the United States, yet its laws concerning brain death manage to be far more protective of both majority and minority perspectives on death while openly acknowledging why, as a matter of social policy, the concept of brain death has value.

Notes

1. Rosner 1969.
2. Law Dictionary 2011.
3. Keown 2005.
4. Pernick 1999.
5. Baker 1971.
6. Beecher et al. 1968.
7. Beecher et al. 1968, 85.
8. Beecher et al. 1968, 85.
9. Beecher et al. 1968, 85–6.
10. Beecher et al. 1968, 87.
11. Rosner 1969.
12. Shewmon 1998; Shewmon 2018.
13. President's Commission 1981, 3.
14. President's Commission 1981, 15.
15. President's Commission 1981.
16. Uniform Law Commission 1980, 5. From 2020 to 2023, the Uniform Law Commission considered revisions to the UDDA to address two problems: ongoing controversy about brain death, and the gulf between clinical practice and the letter of the law that has resulted in clinical determinations of brain death no longer satisfying statutory requirements for whole brain death in the United States. The Commission debated the revisions at its most recent annual meeting in July 2023, and decided to pause the revision process, and make no changes.
17. Wahlster et al. 2015.
18. Lewis et al. 2020.
19. Greer et al. 2016.
20. The new AAN guidelines by Greer et al. 2023 replace the previous guidelines by Wijdicks et al. 2010. A significant change is that the previous guidelines were for adult patients, whereas the new guidelines encompass both adults and children, and thus also replace the guidelines for pediatric patients.
21. The previous guidelines for infants and children were established by the Society of Critical Care Medicine, the American Academy of Pediatrics, and the Child Neurology Society, see Nakagawa et al. 2011.
22. Halevy & Brody 1993; Shewmon 2001; Nair-Collins & Joffe 2021.
23. Wahlster et al. 2015; Shemie et al. 2023.
24. Academy of Royal Medical Colleges 2010, 12.
25. Academy of Royal Medical Colleges 2010, 11.
26. Academy of Royal Medical Colleges 2010, 11.
27. Academy of Royal Medical Colleges 2010, 11.
28. Shemie et al. 2023.
29. Shemie et al. 2023, 484.
30. Shemie et al. 2023, 483.

31. Shemie et al. 2023, 483–4.
32. Shemie et al. 2023, 485.
33. Shemie et al. 2023, 484.
34. Veatch & Ross 2016, 94.
35. Warren 1997; McMahan 1998.
36. Shewmon 1997.
37. Green & Wikler 1980, 127.
38. Veatch 2005.
39. Veatch & Ross 2016, 96.
40. Giacino et al. 2018; Johnson 2022.
41. Johnson 2022.
42. Bernat 2002.
43. Beecher et al. 1968.
44. Johnson 2022, 60.
45. Turgeon et al. 2011; Izzy et al. 2013; Johnson 2016; Johnson 2022.
46. Hansen & Joffe 2017; Shewmon 2017; Latorre, Schmidt, & Greer 2020.
47. Schofield et al. 2015, 605.
48. Scalea et al. 2016; Nair-Collins 2018; Peled et al. 2022; Johnson 2023.
49. Veatch 2019.
50. Fields 2013.
51. Truog 2018.
52. Aviv 2018.
53. Aviv 2018.
54. Aviv 2018.
55. Aviv 2018.
56. Aviv 2018.
57. Shewmon & Salamon 2021, 457.
58. Shewmon 1998.
59. Shewmon 2018.
60. Shewmon 2018; Shewmon & Salamon 2022.
61. Shewmon 2018; Shewmon & Salamon 2022.
62. Aviv 2018.
63. Wijdicks et al. 2010.
64. Wijdicks et al. 2010, 1916.
65. Johnson 2022, 77.
66. Dalia et al. 2019.
67. Dall Ave, Sulmasy, & Bernat 2020.
68. Dall Ave, Sulmasy, & Bernat 2020.
69. Dall Ave, Sulmasy, & Bernat 2020.
70. Joffe 2023, 183.
71. Bernat 2023, 35.
72. Sisk & Foster 2004.
73. Moon & Hyun 2017.
74. Wijdicks et al. 2010; Shemie et al. 2023.
75. Coimbra 1999; Latorre, Schmidt, & Greer 2020; Shewmon 2022.
76. Shewmon 2021.

77. Bernat, Culver, & Gert 1981, 391.
78. Bernat 1984, 48.
79. Bernat 2002, 344.
80. Nair-Collins 2015, 73–4.
81. Shewmon 2001.
82. Shewmon 2001, 465.
83. President's Council on Bioethics 2008, 90.
84. President's Council on Bioethics 2008, 61.
85. President's Council on Bioethics 2008, 35–6.
86. President's Council on Bioethics 2008, 60.
87. President's Council on Bioethics 2008, 63.
88. President's Council on Bioethics 2008, 63.
89. Shewmon 2009, 22.
90. Lewis et al. 2019; Varelas 2023.
91. Lewis, Bonnie, & Pope 2019, 143.
92. Bernat 2023, 33.
93. Saper & Lowell 2014, R11111.
94. Institute of Medicine 1992, 16.
95. Institute of Medicine 1992, 16.
96. Nair-Collins & Miller 2022, 2.
97. Shewmon 2021, 3.
98. Bernat 2023, 33.
99. Bernat 2023, 33.
100. Bernat 2023, 33–4.
101. Truog & Tasker 2017, 702.
102. Berkowitz & Garrett 2020, 4.
103. Jeret & Benjamin 1994; Saposnik, Rizzo, & Deluca 2000; Scott et al. 2013; Sveen et al. 2023.
104. Truog & Tasker 2017, 702–3.
105. Joffe, Anton, & Duff 2010.
106. Joffe, Anton, & Duff 2010, 1437.
107. Lewis & Greer 2017b.
108. Pope 2023b.
109. Berkowitz & Garrett 2020, 5.
110. Truog & Tasker 2017, 703.
111. Berkowitz & Garrett 2020, 10.
112. Johnson 2020, 34.
113. Lewis & Greer 2017a.
114. Bryant 2022.
115. Bryant 2022.
116. Truog & Tasker 2017; Lewis & Greer 2017a; Berkowitz & Garrett 2020.
117. Shewmon 2021, 20.
118. Council of Europe 2013; Seifi, Lacci, & Godoy 2020.
119. Johnson 2023a, 471.
120. Johnson 2023a, 469.
121. Johnson 2023a, 470.

122. McAndrew 2016.
123. Uniform Law Commission 1980, 5.
124. Gebreyes v Prime Healthcare 2015.
125. NRS 451.008.
126. NRS 451.008.
127. Beecher et al. 1968.
128. President's Commission 1981.
129. Academy of Royal Medical Colleges 2010.
130. Academy of Royal Medical Colleges 2010.
131. Johnson 2023a, 468.
132. Johnson 2023a, 470.
133. Nair-Collins 2015, 73.
134. Shah & Miller 2010.
135. Truog & Miller 2014, 10.
136. Shah 2014, 116.
137. Shah 2014, 119.
138. Shah 2014.
139. Shah 2014, 126.
140. Shah 2014, 131.
141. Johnson 2017, 269.
142. Shah 2014, 132.
143. Johnson 2023a, 474.
144. Truog 2023, 701.
145. Paquette et al. 2023, 633.
146. Johnson 2020, 33.
147. Johnson 2020, 33.
148. Wojtasiewicz 2006.
149. Wicher & Meeker 2012; Rubin, Dhar, & Diringer 2014; Hornor et al. 2018.
150. Johnson 2020, 33.
151. Johnson 2023a, 473.
152. Johnson 2023a, 472.
153. Academy of Royal Medical Colleges 2010; Veatch & Ross 2016.
154. Rubin, Dhar, & Diringer 2014; Hornor et al. 2018; Ross 2023.
155. Johnson 2023b.
156. DeCamp, Sulmasy, & Fins 2022; James et al. 2022; Peled et al. 2022; Ross 2023.
157. Truog & Miller 2008, 675.
158. Manning 2013.
159. Crane 2013.
160. Manning 2013.
161. O'Connor v Community Hospital 2020.
162. Jacobs v. Ctr for Organ Recovery & Educ., 2012.
163. Shah, Kasper, & Miller 2015, 1.
164. Shah, Kasper, & Miller 2015, 2.
165. Health Resources & Services Administration 2019.

166. Shah, Kasper, & Miller 2015, 4.
167. Health Resources & Services Administration 2019.
168. Seifi, Lacci, & Godoy 2020; Council of Europe 2013.
169. Terunuma & Mathis 2021, 5.
170. Shroff & Navin 2018, 2.
171. Johnson 2023a, 474.
172. Johnson 2023a, 474.
173. Johnson 2016, 111.
174. Johnson 2023a, 475.
175. Veatch 2019.
176. Veatch & Ross 2016, 106.
177. A (A Child), Re (Rev 1) [2015] EWHC 443 (Fam).
178. A (A Child), Re (Rev 1) [2015] EWHC 443 (Fam).
179. A (A Child), Re (Rev 1) [2015] EWHC 443 (Fam).
180. A (A Child), Re (Rev 1) [2015] EWHC 443 (Fam).
181. A (A Child), Re (Rev 1) [2015] EWHC 443 (Fam).
182. A (A Child), Re (Rev 1) [2015] EWHC 443 (Fam).
183. Brierly 2015, 2254.
184. Donnelly & Lyons 2023, 356.
185. Dyer 2020.
186. Choong & Rady 2018, 74.
187. Choong & Rady 2018, 72.
188. Choong & Rady 2018, 86.
189. Donnelly & Lyons 2023, 356.
190. Donnelly & Lyons 2023, 359.
191. Donnelly & Lyons 2023, 360.
192. King 2013.
193. Donaldson & King 2019; Lavorgna & Hutton 2019.
194. A (A Child), Re (Rev 1) [2015] EWHC 443 (Fam).
195. Beecher et al. 1968.
196. Beecher et al. 1968, 86.
197. Kaechele & Chakko 2023.
198. Coimbra 1999; Shewmon & Salamon 2021.
199. Latorre, Schmidt, & Greer 2020.
200. Shewmon 1998.
201. Johnson 2022.
202. Siminoff, Burant, & Younger 2004.
203. Larue et al. 2013.
204. Shah 2014.
205. NRS 451.007.
206. Pope 2023a.
207. Donnelly & Lyons 2023.
208. Son & Setta 2018.
209. Johnson 2017, 269.
210. Johnson 2023a, 475.
211. Johnson 2017, 269.

212. Manchester University NHS Foundation Trust v Midrar Namiq 2020.
213. Schofield et al. 2015; Shewmon 2017; Latorr, Schmidt, & Greer 2020.
214. Morioka 2001, 42.
215. Terunuma & Mathis 2021, 5.
216. Morioka 2001, 44.
217. Yang & Miller 2015, 219–20.
218. Morioka 2001, 43.
219. Health Resources & Services Administration 2019.

References

A (A Child), Re (Rev 1) [2015] EWHC 443 (Fam) [Internet]. 2015 [cited August 26, 2023]. www.bailii.org/ew/cases/EWHC/Fam/2015/443.html.

Academy of Medical Royal Colleges. A Code of Practice for the Diagnosis and Confirmation of Death [Internet]. Academy of Medical Royal Colleges. 2010 [cited August 8, 2023]. www.aomrc.org.uk/reports-guidance/ukdec-reports-and-guidance/code-practice-diagnosis-confirmation-death/.

Aviv R. What Does It Mean to Die? The New Yorker. January 28, 2018.

Baker AB. Artificial respiration, the history of an idea. Medical History. October 1971;15(4):336–51.

Beecher H, Adams R, Barger C, et al. A definition of irreversible coma: Report of the Ad Hoc Committee of the Harvard Medical School to examine the definition of brain death. JAMA. 1968;205(6):337–40.

Berkowitz I, Garrett J. Legal and ethical considerations for requiring consent for apnea testing in brain death declaration. American Journal of Bioethics. 2020;20(6):4–16.

Bernat JL. Challenges to brain death in revising the Uniform Determination of Death Act: The UDDA revision series. Neurology. July 4, 2023;101(1):30–7.

Bernat JL. The biophilosophical basis of whole-brain death. Social Philosophy & Policy. 2002;19(2):324.

Bernat JL. The definition, criterion, and statute of death. Seminars in Neurology. 1984;4(1):45–51.

Bernat JL, Culver CM, Gert B. On the definition and criterion of death. Annals of Internal Medicine. 1981;94(3):389–94.

Brierley J. UK court accepts neurological determination of death. The Lancet. 2015;385(9984):2254.

Bryant M. Archie Battersbee Case: A Timeline of Key Events. August 6, 2022; www.theguardian.com/uk-news/2022/aug/06/archie-battersbee-case-timeline-key-events-life-support-what-happened.

Busch E, Mjaaland M. Does controlled donation after circulatory death violate the dead donor rule? American Journal of Bioethics. 2023;23(2):4–11.

Choong KA, Rady MY. Re A (a child) and the United Kingdom code of practice for the diagnosis and confirmation of death: Should a secular construct of death override religious values in a pluralistic society? HEC Forum. 2018;30:71–89.

Coimbra CG. Implications of ischemic penumbra for the diagnosis of brain death. Brazilian Journal of Medical and Biological Research. 1999;32:1479–87.

Council of Europe. Organ Shortage: Current Status and Strategies for Improvement of Organ Donation-A European Consensus Document. 2013. www.edqm.eu/

documents/52006/290116/Organ+Shortage+Current+Status+and+Strategies +for+the+Improvement+of+Organ+Donation.pdf/efcf120d-ebb4-0cda-751d- e38b50b0f2f1?version=1.1&t=1643376448578&download=true

Crane M. Dispute over organ donation brings attention to defining death. 2013. The Columbus Dispatch. [cited August 19, 2023]. www.dispatch.com/story/ lifestyle/faith/2013/07/22/dispute-over-organ-donation-brings/23321 596007/.

Dalia AA, Ortoleva J, Fiedler A, et al. Extracorporeal membrane oxygen- ation is a team sport: Institutional survival benefits of a formalized ECMO team. Journal of Cardiothoracic and Vascular Anesthesia. 2019;33 (4):902–7.

Dalle Ave AL, Sulmasy DP, Bernat JL. The ethical obligation of the dead donor rule. Medicine, Health Care and Philosophy. 2020;23(1):43–50.

DeCamp M, Sulmasy LS, Fins JJ. POINT: Does normothermic regional perfu- sion violate the ethical principles underlying organ procurement? Yes. Chest. 2022;162(2):288–90.

Donaldson B, King A. Feeling Animal Death: Being Host to Ghosts. London: Rowman & Littlefield; 2019.

Donnelly M, Lyons B. Disputing death: Brain death in the courts. Legal Studies. June 2023;43(2):351–69.

Dyer C. Baby at centre of legal battle can have life support removed, says judge. BMJ. January 29, 2020;368:m354.

Fields L. ABC News. 2013. [cited August 9, 2023]. Mom of Girl on Life Support: "I Can't Let Them Kill My Baby a Second Time." https://abcnews.go.com/US/ mom-girl-life-support-kill-baby-time/story?id=21305193.

Ford D. Jahi McMath's family seeks to move brain-dead girl to another facility. CNN. 2013 [cited August 9, 2023]. www.cnn.com/2013/12/26/health/jahi- mcmath-girl-brain-dead/index.html.

Gebreyes v. Prime Healthcare Servs., LLC (In re Guardianship of the Pers. & Estate of Hailu) [Internet]. 2015. www.thaddeuspope.com/images/ Aden_Hailu_Nev_11-2015_.pdf.

Giacino JT, Katz DI, Schiff ND, et al. Practice guideline update recommenda- tions summary: Disorders of consciousness: Report of the guideline devel- opment, dissemination, and implementation subcommittee of the American Academy of Neurology; the American Congress of Rehabilitation Medicine; and the National Institute on Disability, Independent Living, and Rehabilitation Research. Archives of Physical Medicine and Rehabilitation. September 1, 2018;99(9):1699–709.

Green MB, Wikler D. Brain death and personal identity. Philosophy & Public Affairs. 1980;9(2):105–33.

Greer DM, Kirschen MP, Lewis A, et al. Pediatric and adult brain death/death by neurologic criteria consensus guideline: Report of the AAN guidelines subcommittee, AAP, CNS, and SCCM. Neurology. October 11, 2023;101 (24):1112–32.

Greer DM, Wang HH, Robinson JD, et al. Variability of brain death policies in the United States. JAMA Neurology. 2016;73(2):213–8.

Halevy A, Brody B. Brain death: Reconciling definitions, criteria, and tests. Annals of Internal Medicine. 1993;119(6):519–25.

Hansen G, Joffe AR. Confounding brain stem function during pediatric brain death determination: Two case reports. Journal of Child Neurology. 2017;32 (7):676–9.

Health Resources & Services Administration. 2019. National Survey of Organ Donation Attitudes and Practices [Internet]. [cited August 19, 2023]. https:// data.hrsa.gov/topics/health-systems/organ_donation_opinion_survey-data.

Hornor MA, Byrne JP, Engelhardt KE, Nathens AB. Examining racial disparities in the time to withdrawal of life-sustaining treatment in trauma. Journal of Trauma and Acute Care Surgery. 2018;84(4):590–7.

Institute of Medicine and National Academy of Sciences. Discovering the Brain. Washington, DC: National Academies Press; 1992.

Izzy S, Compton R, Carandang R, Hall W, Muehlschlegel S. Self-fulfilling prophecies through withdrawal of care: Do they exist in traumatic brain injury, too? Neurocritical Care. 2013;19(3):347–63.

Jacobs v. Ctr. for Organ Recovery & Educ., Case No. 1:09-cv-48-SJM (W.D. Pa. November 6, 2012).

James L, Parent B, Moazami N, Smith DE. Counterpoint: Does normothermic regional perfusion violate the ethical principles underlying organ procurement? No. Chest. 2022;162(2):290–2.

Jeret JS, Benjamin JL. Risk of hypotension during apnea testing. Archives of Neurology. 1994;51(6):595–9.

Joffe AR. Should the criterion for brain death require irreversible or permanent cessation of function? Irreversible: The UDDA revision series. Neurology. July 25, 2023;101(4):181–3.

Joffe AR, Anton NR, Duff JP. The apnea test: Rationale, confounders, and criticism. Journal of Child Neurology. 2010;25(11):1435–43.

Johnson LSM. The case for reasonable accommodation of conscientious objections to declarations of brain death. Journal of Bioethical Inquiry. 2016;13 (1):105–15.

Johnson LSM. Inference and inductive risk in disorders of consciousness. AJOB Neuroscience. January 2, 2016;7(1):35–43.

Johnson LSM. Death by neurological criteria: Expert definitions and lay misgivings. QJM: An International Journal of Medicine. May 1, 2017;110 (5):267–70.

Johnson LSM. Restoring trust and requiring consent in death by neurological criteria. The American Journal of Bioethics. 2020;20(6):33–5.

Johnson LSM. The Ethics of Uncertainty: Entangled Ethical and Epistemic Risks in Disorders of Consciousness. New York: Oxford University Press; 2022.

Johnson LSM. Arguments favoring continuation of "organ support" when families object to declaration of death by neurologic criteria. In Lewis A, Bernat JL, editors. Death Determination by Neurologic Criteria: Areas of Controversy and Consensus. 2023a. Cham, Switzerland: Springer;467–77.

Johnson LSM. DCD donors are dying, but not dead. The American Journal of Bioethics. February 1, 2023b;23(2):28–30.

Kaechele AP, Chakko MN. Nuclear medicine cerebral perfusion scan. [Updated August 21, 2023]. In StatPearls [Internet]. Treasure Island (FL): StatPearls; 2023. www.ncbi.nlm.nih.gov/books/NBK582135/#

Keown D. End of life: The Buddhist view. The Lancet. 2005;366(9489):952–5.

King BJ. How Animals Grieve. Chicago: University of Chicago Press; 2013.

Larue C, DeJong J, Schlosser MP, et al. A survey to determine public opinion regarding whether brain death is death and should allow vital organ donation. In: C54 Patients, Ethics and End of Life Care. American Thoracic Society. 2013;187:A4433.

Latorre JGS, Schmidt EB, Greer DM. Another pitfall in brain death diagnosis: Return of cerebral function after determination of brain death by both clinical and radionuclide cerebral perfusion imaging. Neurocritical Care. 2020;32:1–7.

Lavorgna BF, Hutton VE. Grief severity: A comparison between human and companion animal death. Death Studies. 2019;43(8):521–6.

Law Dictionary [Internet]. 2011 [cited August 8, 2023]. Death: Definition & Meaning – Black's Law Dictionary. https://thelawdictionary.org/death/.

Lewis A, Bakkar A, Kreiger-Benson E, et al. Determination of death by neurologic criteria around the world. Neurology. 2020;95(3):e299–309.

Lewis A, Bonnie RJ, Pope T. It's time to revise the Uniform Determination of Death Act. Annals of Internal Medicine. July 7, 2020;173(1):75–6.

Lewis A, Bonnie RJ, Pope T, et al. Determination of death by neurologic criteria in the United States: The case for revising the Uniform Determination of Death Act. The Journal of Law, Medicine & Ethics. 2019;47(4_suppl):9–24.

Lewis A, Greer D. Point: Should informed consent be required for apnea testing in patients with suspected brain death? No. Chest. 2017a;152(4):700–2.

Lewis A, Greer D. Rebuttal from Drs Lewis and Greer. Chest. 2017b;152 (4):704–5.

Manchester University NHS Foundation Trust. v Midrar Namiq, Mr Karwan Mohammed Ali and Ms Shokhan Namiq. [2020] EWHC 5 (Fam) [Internet]. 2020. www.judiciary.uk/wp-content/uploads/2020/01/Midrar-Namiq-Approved-Judgment.pdf.

Manning A. Family loses fight to keep son's organs from donation. 2013. The Columbus Dispatch [Internet]. [cited August 14, 2023]. www.dispatch.com/story/news/crime/2013/07/11/family-loses-fight-to-keep/24114454007/.

Marquis D. Are DCD donors dead? The Hastings Center Report. 2010;40(3):24–31.

McAndrew S. The contested death of Aden Hailu. Reno Gazette-Journal. March 25, 2016. www.rgj.com/story/news/2016/03/25/contested-death-aden-hailu/82269006/

McMahan J. Brain death, cortical death, and persistent vegetative state. In Singer P, Kuhe H, editors. A Companion to Bioethics. Hoboken: Wiley & Sons, 2009.

Moon JW, Hyun DK. Chronic brain-dead patients who exhibit Lazarus sign. Korean J Neurotrauma. October 2017;13(2):153–7.

Morioka M. Reconsidering brain death: A lesson from Japan's fifteen years of experience. Hastings Center Report. 2001;31(4):41–6.

Nair-Collins M. An unquestioned assumption in the debate on the dead donor rule. Journal of Medical Ethics. 2018;44(12):872–3.

Nair-Collins M. Clinical and ethical perspectives on brain death. Medicolegal and Bioethics. 2015; 5: 69–80.

Nair-Collins M, Joffe AR. Hypothalamic function in patients diagnosed as brain dead and its practical consequences. Handbook of Clinical Neurology. 2021;182:433–46.

Nair-Collins M, Miller FG. Current practice diagnosing brain death is not consistent with legal statutes requiring the absence of all brain function. Journal of Intensive Care Medicine. 2022;37(2):153–6.

Nakagawa TA, Ashwal S, Mathur M, Mysore M. Guidelines for the determination of brain death in infants and children: An update of the 1987 Task Force recommendations. Pediatrics. September 1, 2011;128(3):e720–40.

NRS 451.007. Nevada Revised Statutes Chapter 451 – Dead Bodies – Requirements for Determination. [Internet]. NV Rev Stat § 451.007 (2019), 451.007. www.leg.state.nv.us/nrs/nrs-451.html#NRS451Sec008.

NRS 451.008. NRS: Chapter 451 – Dead Bodies [Internet]. www.leg.state.nv.us/nrs/nrs-451.html#NRS451Sec008.

O'Connor v Community Hospital 2020. Appellant's Opening Brief in the Court of Appeal of the State of California in and for the Fifth Appellate District

[Internet]. www.thaddeuspope.com/images/O_CONNOR_v._COMMUNITY_ HOSP._MED._CTR.pdf.

Paquette ED, Ross LF, Chavez J, Frader JE. Refusals of the determination of death by neurologic criteria: A mixed methods study of physician perspectives on refusals cases. Pediatric Critical Care Medicine. 2023;24(8):628–35.

Peled H, Mathews S, Rhodes D, Bernat JL. Normothermic regional perfusion requires careful ethical analysis before adoption into donation after circulatory determination of death. Critical Care Medicine. November 2022;50-(11):1644–8.

Pernick MS. Brain death in a cultural context: The reconstruction of death, 1967–1981. In Youngner SJ, Arnold RM, Shapiro R, editors. The Definition of Death: Contemporary Controversies. 1999. Baltimore: Johns Hopkins University Press;3–33.

Pope TM. Brain Death Resources. 2023a. [cited August 27, 2023]. www .thaddeuspope.com/braindeath.html.

Pope TM. Consent for Brain Death Testing [Internet]. 2023b. [cited August 14, 2023]. www.thaddeuspope.com/braindeath/apneaconsent.html.

President's Commission for the Study of Ethical Problems in Medicine and Biomedical and Behavioral Research. Defining Death: A Report on the Medical, Legal and Ethical Issues in the Determination of Death. Washington, DC: President's Commission for the Study of Ethical Problems in Medicine and Biomedical and Behavioral Research; 1981.

President's Council on Bioethics. Controversies in the Determination of Death: A White Paper of the President's Council on Bioethics. 2008. Washington, DC.

Quality Standards Subcommittee of the American Academy of Neurology. Practice parameters for determining brain death in adults (summary statement). Neurology. 1995;45:1012–4.

Rosner F. The definition of death in Jewish law. Tradition: A Journal of Orthodox Jewish Thought. 1969;10(4):33–9.

Ross LF. The dead donor rule does require that the donor is dead. The American Journal of Bioethics. February 1, 2023;23(2):12–4.

Rubin MA, Dhar R, Diringer MN. Racial differences in withdrawal of mechanical ventilation do not alter mortality in neurologically injured patients. Journal of Critical Care. 2014;29(1):49–53.

Saper CB, Lowell BB. The hypothalamus. Current Biology. 2014;24(23): R1111–6.

Saposnik G, Rizzo G, Deluca JL. Pneumothorax and pneumoperitoneum during the apnea test: How safe is this procedure? Arquivos de Neuro-Psiquiatria. 2000;58:905–8.

Scalea JR, Redfield RR, Rizzari MD, et al. When do DCD donors die? Annals of Surgery. 2016;263(2):211–6.

Schofield GM, Urch CE, Stebbing J, Giamas G. When does a human being die? QJM: An International Journal of Medicine. August 1, 2015;108 (8):605–9.

Scott JB, Gentile MA, Bennett SN, Couture M, MacIntyre NR. Apnea testing during brain death assessment: A review of clinical practice and published literature. Respiratory Care. 2013;58(3):532–8.

Seifi A, Lacci JV, Godoy DA. Incidence of brain death in the United States. Clinical Neurology and Neurosurgery. August 1, 2020;195:105885.

Shah SK. Piercing the veil: The limits of brain death as a legal fiction. University of Michigan Journal of Law Reform. 2014;48:301.

Shah SK, Kasper K, Miller FG. A narrative review of the empirical evidence on public attitudes on brain death and vital organ transplantation: The need for better data to inform policy. Journal of Medical Ethics. 2015;41(4):291–6.

Shah SK, Miller FG. Can we handle the truth? Legal fictions in the determination of death. American Journal of Law & Medicine. 2010;36(4):540–85.

Shemie SD, Wilson LC, Hornby L, et al. A brain-based definition of death and criteria for its determination after arrest of circulation or neurologic function in Canada: A 2023 clinical practice guideline. Canadian Journal of Anesthesia/Journal canadien d'anesthésie. April 1, 2023;70(4):483–557.

Shewmon DA. Brain death: Can it be resuscitated? The Hastings Center Report. 2009;39(2):18–24.

Shewmon DA. Chronic "brain death": Meta-analysis and conceptual consequences. Neurology. 1998;51(6):1538–45.

Shewmon DA. False-positive diagnosis of brain death following the pediatric guidelines: Case report and discussion. Journal of Child Neurology. 2017;32 (14):1104–17.

Shewmon DA. Recovery from "brain death": A neurologist's apologia. The Linacre Quarterly. 1997;64(1):30–96.

Shewmon DA. Statement in support of revising the Uniform Determination of Death Act and in opposition to a proposed revision. The Journal of Medicine and Philosophy: A Forum for Bioethics and Philosophy of Medicine. 2021;48(5):453–77.

Shewmon DA. The brain and somatic integration: Insights into the standard biological rationale for equating "brain death" with death. The Journal of Medicine and Philosophy: A Forum for Bioethics and Philosophy of Medicine. January 1, 2001;26(5):457–78.

Shewmon DA. The case of Jahi McMath: A neurologist's view. Hastings Center Report. 2018;48(S4):S74–6.

Shewmon DA. Truly reconciling the case of Jahi McMath. Neurocritical Care. October 1, 2018;29(2):165–70.

Shewmon DA, Salamon N. The extraordinary case of Jahi McMath. Perspectives in Biology and Medicine. 2021;64(4):457–78.

Shewmon DA, Salamon N. The MRI of Jahi McMath and its implications for the global ischemic penumbra hypothesis. Journal of Child Neurology. 2022;37(1):35–42.

Shroff S, Navin S. "Brain death" and "circulatory death": Need for a uniform definition of death in India. The Indian Journal of Medical Ethics. 2018;3 (4):321–3.

Siminoff LA, Burant C, Youngner SJ. Death and organ procurement: Public beliefs and attitudes. Social Science & Medicine. 2004;59(11):2325–34.

Sisk CL, Foster DL. The neural basis of puberty and adolescence. Nature Neuroscience. 2004;7(10):1040–7.

Son RG, Setta SM. Frequency of use of the religious exemption in New Jersey cases of determination of brain death. BMC Medical Ethics. August 14, 2018;19(1):76.

Sveen WN, Antommaria AHM, Gilene SJ, Stalets EL. Adverse events during apnea testing for the determination of death by neurologic criteria: A single-center, retrospective pediatric cohort. Pediatric Critical Care Medicine. 2023;24:399–405.

Terunuma Y, Mathis BJ. Cultural sensitivity in brain death determination: A necessity in end-of-life decisions in Japan. BMC Medical Ethics. 2021;22(1):1–6.

Truog RD. Lessons from the case of Jahi McMath. Hastings Center Report. 2018;48(S4):S70–3.

Truog RD. Why do families reject the diagnosis of brain death, and how should we respond? Pediatric Critical Care Medicine. August 2023;24(8):701.

Truog RD, Miller FG. Changing the conversation about brain death. The American Journal of Bioethics. 2014;14(8):9–14.

Truog RD, Miller FG. The dead donor rule and organ transplantation. The New England Journal of Medicine. 2008;359(7):674–5.

Truog RD, Tasker RC. Counterpoint: Should informed consent be required for apnea testing in patients with suspected brain death? Yes. Chest. 2017;152 (4):702–4.

Turgeon AF, Lauzier F, Simard JF, et al. Mortality associated with withdrawal of life-sustaining therapy for patients with severe traumatic brain injury: A Canadian multicentre cohort study. Canadian Medical Association Journal. 2011;183(14):1581–8.

Uniform Law Commission. Uniform Determination of Death Act 1980 [Internet]. [cited August 8, 2023]. www.uniformlaws.org/viewdocument/final-act-49?CommunityKey=155faf5d-03c2-4027-99ba-ee4c99019d6c&tab=librarydocuments.

Varelas PN. Must hypothalamic neurosecretory function cease for brain death determination? No: The UDDA revision series. Neurology. July 18, 2023;101(3):137–9.

Veatch RM. Controversies in defining death: A case for choice. Theoretical Medicine and Bioethics. 2019;40(5):381–401.

Veatch RM. The death of whole-brain death: The plague of the disaggregators, somaticists, and mentalists. Journal of Medicine and Philosophy. August 1, 2005;30(4):353–78.

Veatch RM, Ross LF. Defining Death: The Case for Choice. Washington, DC: Georgetown University Press; 2016.

Wahlster S, Wijdicks EF, Patel PV, et al. Brain death declaration practices and perceptions worldwide. Neurology. 2015;84(18):1870–9.

Warren MA. Moral Status: Obligations to Persons and Other Living Things. Oxford: Clarendon Press; 1997.

Wicher CP, Meeker MA. What influences African American end-of-life preferences? Journal of Health Care for the Poor and Underserved. 2012;23(1):28–58.

Wijdicks EFM, Varelas PN, Gronseth GS, Greer DM. Evidence-based guideline update: Determining brain death in adults. Report of the Quality Standards Subcommittee of the American Academy of Neurology. 2010;74(23):1911–8.

Wojtasiewicz ME. Damage compounded: Disparities, distrust, and disparate impact in end-of-life conflict resolution policies. The American Journal of Bioethics. 2006;6(5):8–12.

Yang Q, Miller G. East–west differences in perception of brain death. Journal of Bioethical Inquiry. June 1, 2015;12(2):211–25.

Cambridge Elements ☰

Bioethics and Neuroethics

Thomasine Kushner
California Pacific Medical Center, San Francisco

Thomasine Kushner, PhD, is the founding Editor of the *Cambridge Quarterly of Healthcare Ethics* and coordinates the International Bioethics Retreat, where bioethicists share their current research projects, the Cambridge Consortium for Bioethics Education, a growing network of global bioethics educators, and the Cambridge-ICM Neuroethics Network, which provides a setting for leading brain scientists and ethicists to learn from each other.

About the Series
Bioethics and neuroethics play pivotal roles in today's debates in philosophy, science, law, and health policy. With the rapid growth of scientific and technological advances, their importance will only increase. This series provides focused and comprehensive coverage in both disciplines consisting of foundational topics, current subjects under discussion and views toward future developments.

Cambridge Elements ≡

Bioethics and Neuroethics

Printed in the United States
by Baker & Taylor Publisher Services